Praise for *Dear Digital, We need to talk*

'Finally, a pragmatic book that helps you take back control of those wayward tech habits and helps knowledge workers thrive in a world of digital distractions.'

Dominic Price | Work Futurist at Atlassian and TED speaker

'Kristy's work stands out as the perfect blend of art and science – solidly evidence-based and masterfully relatable. She patiently takes the reader through the "why" of our habits and behaviours before sharing how to adapt. Don't put this book on your holiday reading pile; read it now and start living a higher-resolution life.'

Katherine Milesi | Strategic Advisor, Digital Transformation, Deloitte Asia Pacific

'*Dear Digital, We need to talk* is a really practical guide to empowering yourself to use technology in a mindful and intentional way. It's full of science-backed tips you can put in place today to make technology work for you.'

Sophie Scott | Adjunct Associate Professor, University of Notre Dame Australia; author; speaker | sophiescott.com.au

'Dr Kristy has written a fabulous book that we all need as we navigate living, working and parenting in this digital age. She weaves the science with a good dose of common sense and humour and most importantly, she gives doable strategies that can tame technology.'

Maggie Dent | Bestselling parenting author, educator and host of ABC's *Parental as Anything* podcast

A GUILT-FREE GUIDE TO TAMING YOUR TECH HABITS AND THRIVING IN A DISTRACTED WORLD

Dr Kristy Goodwin

MACMILLAN

First published in 2023 by Major Street Publishing Pty Ltd

First published in India 2023 by Macmillan
an imprint of Pan Macmillan Publishing India Private Limited
707 Kailash Building
26 K. G. Marg, New Delhi 110001
www.panmacmillan.co.in

Pan Macmillan, The Smithson, 6 Briset Street, Farringdon, London EC1M 5NR
Associated companies throughout the world
www.panmacmillan.com

ISBN 978-93-95624-91-6

1 3 5 7 9 8 6 4 2

Internal design by Production Works
Printed in India Gopsons Papers Pvt. Ltd., Noida.

Contents

About the author

Having personally experienced how our always-on digital culture is compromising people's wellbeing and is counter to optimal and sustainable performance, award-winning researcher and speaker Dr Kristy Goodwin is on a mission to promote employee wellbeing and bolster workplace productivity in an always-on digital world.

As a digital wellbeing and productivity expert, she shares practical, brain-based hacks to tame tech habits, along with the latest evidence-based strategies to decode the neurobiology of peak performance in the technological era.

Dr Kristy is regularly called on by the media for her expert opinion on how our digitalised lives are impacting our focus and wellbeing. She translates the latest research into realistic strategies to help people tame their tech habits, without suggesting that we cancel Zoom meetings, go on a digital detox or cancel our Netflix subscriptions.

Senior business leaders and HR executives from Australia's top organisations engage Dr Kristy to help them promote employee digital wellbeing and performance. Her roster of clients includes Apple, AMP, Deutsche Bank, Bank of Queensland, Challenger, Westpac, DLA Piper, McDonald's, Scentre Group, Randstad, the Reserve Bank of Australia, Cuscal, National Broadband Network and Foxtel.

Dr Kristy delivers keynotes and workshops on stage and online from her professional, custom-built studio. She delivers consultancy services to help organisations establish their digital guardrails: the digital norms, practices and principles that underpin effective and productive use of digital technologies in hybrid or remote settings.

Dr Kristy is on a mission to help people stop being slaves to the screen and thrive in the digital world.

Preface

Warning – your digital diagnosis

Jessica tossed her daughter Harper's school bag in the back of the car, climbed into the driver's seat and winked at her in the rear vision mirror. She started to ask Harper about her day at school when a phone call interjected. She ignored the call, and when the voicemail notification illuminated her screen, she could also see the myriad of other notifications that had accumulated in the short time she'd left her phone in the car to walk into after-school care to pick up Harper. *Not another message*, Jessica thought. Her technostress was rising yet again.

Harper glanced out the window, feeling despondent that her mum's phone had once again diverted her attention. Harper interrupted her mum's spiralling thoughts and foreboding sense of overwhelm. 'Mum, how much do you earn per hour?'

Jessica was as perplexed by Harper's question as she was proud of it. She explained that she earned a salary and would need to do some calculations to answer Harper's question.

Later that night, after dealing with the voicemail issue, triaging her inbox and replying to the multitude of WhatsApp messages that had amassed during the day, she went into Harper's bedroom to read with her and kiss her goodnight. She climbed into Harper's bed and explained that she'd done some calculations to determine her 'hourly rate'. She expected Harper to be impressed by the number, or perhaps to start asking about potential career options.

Instead, Harper turned and said to her mum, 'Okay, I'd like to buy an hour of your time *without* your phone. Now I know how much pocket money I'll need.'

Jessica gasped, held her chest and closed her eyes. This is not how she wanted her daughter to remember her childhood, with her mum – and often her dad – constantly tethered to technology.

Jessica tried to mentally reconcile the stinging words her daughter had innocently said. *She was often on her phone, working, so she could be with Harper at soccer. She was checking emails while cooking dinner. She was doing her makeup and trying to reply to the SMS her friend had sent three days earlier.* However, she knew that her digital load had grown exponentially in recent times – especially since she started to work remotely three days a week – and that, as hard as it was to admit, she was often staring at her phone. Digital intruders had started to creep into *every* crevice of her life.

Jessica's story is not unique. You can likely see yourself in this story or in a similar scenario, even if you don't have children.

Many of us knowledge workers – people who spend the bulk of our workday using a laptop or desktop computer – are spending more time attached to technology. In fact, research indicated that during the COVID-19 pandemic adults were spending an average of 13.28 hours per day on digital devices! It has been estimated that the average Australian will spend almost 17 years of their life on their phone, equating to around 33 per cent of their waking hours (see figure 0.1 opposite).

We've become slaves to the screen, both professionally and personally.

Figure 0.1: The Average Aussie's phone use

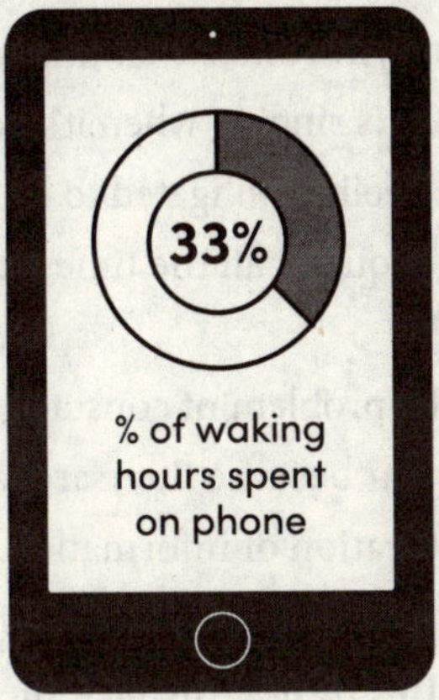

Let's do a quick 'digital diagnosis'. Which of the following conditions and experiences have you encountered?

- **Digital dementia:** The shrinkage of people's memory-making capacity because of digital reliance. Can you remember more than three phone numbers without looking at your phone?
- **Techno-tantrum:** When a 'screenager' who is usually well-adjusted emotionally combusts when digitally disconnected.
- **Email apnoea:** Unconsciously holding your breath or breathing shallowly when responding to emails (or when engaged in other screen activities).
- **Nomophobia:** The fear of not having your phone in close proximity.
- **Toilet tweeting:** Research suggests that up to 40% of adults now use their smartphones while sitting on the loo.
- **Digital burnout:** The depletion of energy, exhaustion, apathy or cynicism towards work, and reduced efficacy resulting from intense digital activity.

- **Digital depletion:** The mental exhaustion resulting from looking at a screen all day.
- **Phantom vibration syndrome:** That tingling feeling that your phone or smartwatch is ringing when it's nowhere near your body.
- **Availability creep:** Feeling obligated to be available and responsive to work requests all the time, including outside work hours.
- **Calendar Tetris:** The problem of constantly needing to shuffle items on your calendar because there are too many of them to fit.
- **Infobesity:** Oversaturation of information. As adults, we're processing 74 gigabytes of data each day, and it's making us ill.
- **Biological buffers (or, rather, the lack thereof):** Sleep, physical movement, breathing, sunlight exposure and connection are buffers baked into our days to help us cope with the stress caused by our tech habits. Are you losing yours?
- **Wired and tired:** Not wanting to switch off or put down that phone. Our digital habits over the entirety of the day are eroding the quality and quantity of our sleep. Revenge bedtime procrastination, anyone?
- **Digital micro-stressors:** The everyday little stressors – emails, text messages, Zoom meetings, alerts and notifications – that might seem quite benign or insignificant but accumulate over time and leave us feeling stressed.
- **Smombie**: 'Smartphone zombie' – a person crossing busy city streets while engrossed in their smartphone or wearing headphones.
- **Tech neck:** Frequent neck pain after a day hunched over your computer.
- **Digital eye strain:** A cluster of symptoms, such as headaches, blurred vision, dry eyes and tech neck, caused by staring at a screen.

- **Meeting bloat:** Too many virtual meetings, caused by the zero cost of inclusion (it's easier to send a calendar invitation to 15 people than to call 15 people to arrange a meeting time).
- **Zoom-bombing:** Unwanted, disruptive intrusions while on video calls (such as partially clothed children and/or partners).

Our unhealthy digital dependencies are having significant impacts on our mental wellbeing, physical health and productivity. Just like Jessica, many of us are feeling digitally depleted and, as a result, we are OUSTED (see figure 0.2).

Figure 0.2: OUSTED

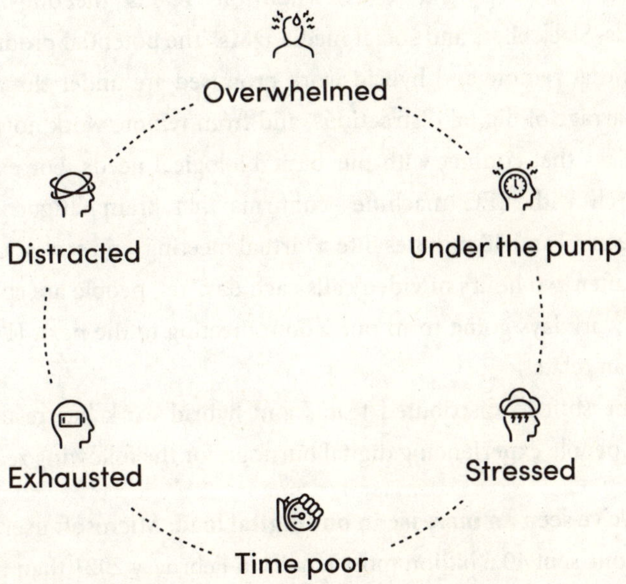

The pandemic ushered in permanent and significant changes to how we work. We've seen radical shifts in how, where and when we work. These changes happened almost instantaneously and without a lot of guidance regarding best practice. Many of us walked out of our office in March 2020 with our laptop under our arm and were thrust into remote work. Microsoft CEO Satya Nadella stated that organisations underwent two years of digital transformation in two months.

The rise of digitisation due to remote work – and now hybrid work – has brought with it a perceived need always to be on, and with that our wellbeing and productivity have taken a hit. We've adopted digital behaviours that are incongruent with our neurobiology – how we as humans actually operate, which is our human operating system (hOS).

This is why many people are experiencing 'digital burnout'. Digital burnout results from unhealthy and unsustainable digital behaviours that leave us feeling stressed. We spend our days bouncing between emails, WhatsApp messages, Microsoft Teams meetings, Trello boards, Slack chats and social media DMs. The potential productivity gains that remote and hybrid work promised are under threat from the barrage of digital distractions, and from remote work norms and practices that conflict with our basic biological needs. For example, research with EEG machines confirms that brain fatigue sets in between 30 and 40 minutes into a virtual meeting, and stress accumulates after two hours of video calls each day. Yet, people are spending their workdays going from one Zoom meeting to the next. (I'm sure you can relate!)

The shift to distributed teams and hybrid work has resulted in more people experiencing digital burnout, for the following reasons:

- **We've seen an increase in our digital load:** Microsoft users alone sent 40.6 billion more emails in February 2021 than they did in February 2020.
- **We've adopted digital work practices that are incongruent with our biological blueprint:** We're spending our days multi-tasking, triaging our inboxes during virtual meetings and working on three projects at once in different tabs. That simply

doesn't work for our brains and bodies – it's draining our brain and denting our productivity!

- **We have an always-on, busy culture:** This culture dominates most workplaces (and did even before the pandemic). Remote work has heightened this culture and created 'digital presenteeism', where your productivity and performance are superficially gauged by how responsive you are to emails or Teams chats.

As we're reconceptualising new ways of working, now is the time for us to map our growing knowledge of how the brain and body work best in a digital context to the work practices and norms we're embedding. Atlassian's Work Futurist, Dominic Price, suggests that we can't superimpose how we once worked in an office environment over how we work remotely, and that we must find new operational cadences and work practices to suit our new ways of working.

Previous books have identified the issues we're facing; our digital dependency, waning attention spans and quest to be productive online have been extensively explored. While these books have certainly started the conversation and raised awareness of the problems we're confronting, few have provided realistic solutions. We need pragmatic solutions so that we can use technology in ways that support, rather than stifle, our wellbeing and productivity (and don't add to our techno-guilt).

Few of us are oblivious to the issues we're facing with technology, as most of us have lived experience of feeling tethered to our phones, or distracted by the pings and dings; but what we hanker for is positive and attainable solutions. This book will arm you with the tangible strategies and tech habits you can apply to your personal and professional life so you can thrive online.

We cannot outperform our neurobiology. We must create a future of work that's grounded in science and psychology, rather than defaulting to assumptions grounded in outdated, industrialised work practices.

This is a paradigm-shifting moment in time. It's the silver-lining of the pandemic: we can now create ways of working that work *with* our brains and bodies, yielding benefits for us as knowledge workers *and* for the organisations we work for.

That's exactly what this book offers. In it, I share simple, science-backed solutions to your most common digital dilemmas.

I don't propose that you digitally amputate yourself (or even worse, if you're a parent of screenagers, that you propose this to your kids or teens). My solutions don't involve planning a #digitaldetox or going 'laptopless'. Digital minimalism is not a relevant or realistic solution for us knowledge workers. Whether we love it or loathe it, technology is here to stay. It plays a vital role in our lives, so we need to develop sustainable digital habits that make work work for us and our workplaces.

Dear Digital, We need to talk shows you that you're feeling OUSTED because technology has its tentacles in every facet of your life. More importantly, it shows you what you can do to tackle it. I share realistic, research-backed strategies that help you thrive online, and I've compiled a menu of micro-habits that you can easily implement to help you do this.

Now, please don't think that I live in a sort of digital utopia and have tamed *my* tech habits. Even as someone who researches, speaks and writes about digital wellbeing and digital distractions, I'm not immune to the 'digital pull'. I self-medicate with some trashy TV after delivering a keynote. (Please don't judge me, but *Selling Sunset* is my tech temptation.) I scroll social media more than I should, especially when I'm tired. (I'll explain why we do this later in the book.) As I share in this book, I've also experienced digital burnout and come out the other side.

There have been times when my tech habits were out of control. In fact, I was once so digitally distracted, dealing with an avalanche of emails, that I wasn't supervising my son, Billy, who was 15 months' old at the time. As I was frantically triaging my inbox, he sustained a serious facial injury after falling face-first off the lounge, requiring hospitalisation.

Thankfully, Billy made a quick recovery. However, he's been left with a scar on his lip. Still, to this day, I look at that little bulge on his lower right lip and feel riddled with intense guilt. *How could I have been so inept? Shouldn't the digital wellbeing expert have more control over her digital behaviours? Why didn't I just open my inbox, send off the cancellation email and shut the lid? Why is the online world so captivating?*

This incident was the catalyst for me to explore why the digital world has such a strong hold on us. In the years prior, my research and speaking work had centred on how screenagers' use of digital devices was shaping their learning, focus and wellbeing. However, Billy's accident forced me to acknowledge that many adults were just as seduced by their screens as their kids were. As adults, many of us have spent years wagging our fingers at kids and teens and declaring that they're 'addicted' but ignored the fact that we're also glued to our screens. We've attempted to justify our unhealthy digital dependencies under the guise that they're essential for our work. But are they really? Or have our digital habits become problematic?

It's time for us to tame our tech habits and take back control of technology: dear digital, we need to talk.

This book will empower you to make informed decisions about how you use technology so you don't let it control you. It's time for you to thrive online.

I am guessing you've never been more ready for this. Am I right?

Kristy

Introduction

Overload – digital burnout!

My relationship with my phone is, well… complicated. It's a little bit like the relationship I have with my husband: hard to live *with* at times but impossible to live *without* (and it's *always* turned on!).

Remember the good old-fashioned days when we'd go and read information in an encyclopaedia? Or when we'd call someone's secretary (do they even exist anymore?) to organise a meeting? Instead, we can often feel like the living example of the head-exploding emoji. Our brains have not evolved to cope with constant digital onslaught. We're literally drowning in information, in what's colloquially being referred to as 'infobesity'.

In 2011, it was estimated that Americans consumed five times as much information daily as they did in 1986 – that's an estimated equivalent of 174 newspapers *every single day*. A 2009 study suggested that adults were consuming 34.7 gigabytes worth of data every single day during their leisure time, which is more than some of our ancestors would have consumed in a lifetime! More recent estimates suggest that it's more than double that – closer to 74 gigabytes worth of data each day.

While the information coming our way has grown exponentially, our brains have not evolved. Our hippocampus – the brain's memory centre, which I liken to our brain's hard drive – has not increased capacity. We cannot load more RAM onto our hippocampus. To cope with our increased digital load, many of us have reverted to multi-tasking, working for long periods and having our days peppered with digital distractions. We've adopted digital habits that are completely incongruent with our neurobiology, with how our brains and bodies work best. As a result, many of us are living in a constant state of stress and distraction. If left unresolved, chronic stress can lead to burnout.

The digital superstorm (aka shitstorm)

There are three colliding factors that explain our digital infatuation:

1. Technology has been designed to fulfil our most basic psychological needs.
2. Persuasive design techniques lure us in.
3. Our digital behaviours cause neurobiological changes.

Technology has been designed to fulfil our most basic psychological needs

According to self-determination theory, we have three basic psychological needs: the need to connect, to feel competent and to feel in control. Our psychological driver to connect explains why we love social media and feel like we need to reply to *every* Teams message that comes our way, and why it can be nearly impossible to ignore the 3 p.m. email that lands in our inbox from our boss on a Saturday. We meet our need to feel competent by immediately replying to a colleague's email, and our digital habits give us a sense of control.

Persuasive design techniques lure us in

If you haven't watched *The Social Dilemma*, I encourage you to do so (after you've read this book). This documentary explores some of the persuasive design techniques that social media uses to hook us. For example, we experience the state of insufficiency online – we never feel 'done' or complete – because there are no stopping cues. There's always another message or email, or another refresh of the social media feed we can do.

Many digital technologies have been designed to function like poker machines and offer us intermittent, variable, randomised rewards, which, in turn, activate the reward pathways of the brain. This releases dopamine, the feel-good hormone, driving us to keep checking our devices. This can cause obsessive and dependent behaviours. If we knew that precisely every two hours and 17 minutes we'd receive a wonderful email, we wouldn't keep checking our inboxes intermittently; it's the unpredictable reward ratio that gets us hooked.

The allocation of likes, shares and comments on social media is what has kept so many of us plugged into these platforms. It's been alleged that some social media platforms have deliberately withdrawn social media vanity metrics such as likes and comments based on a user's demographic profile, because giving them a surge of likes and comments conditions them to constantly check the platform.

Our digital behaviours cause neurobiological changes

When you engage in appealing digital tasks, your brain releases dopamine. The striatum, a part of the brain that's integral to your reward system, encourages you to take the most immediate reward. This is why, when faced with the choice between completing complex data analysis or checking email, the striatum will urge you to take the 'easy route' and jump into your inbox. In turn, dopamine hijacks the frontal lobe of the brain (which would otherwise regulate your behaviour), impairing your capacity to manage your impulses. Therefore, getting stuck in Slack or constantly nibbling at emails throughout the day can become a habitual pattern because of the constant digital dopamine dump.

This also explains why we might start off with the intention to eat one square of chocolate, but one can quickly become two, which becomes half the block – because dopamine overrides the logical part of the brain that would regulate behaviour.

Humans engage in a physiological sigh roughly every five minutes: we perform a double inhalation through the nose, followed by an exhalation through the mouth. This is a biological mechanism that helps us regulate our oxygen and carbon dioxide levels and, through this, our stress response. Sighing supports the biological processes required for stability and resetting arousal states. However, when using screens, we tend to sigh much less, indicating that we're usually more stressed when on our devices.

These are just some of the ways our devices are causing neurobiological changes.

What if *we* are not broken?

In recent years, I've had moments when I've hidden in the bathroom and wondered, *why am I the only one who can't handle the stress? What am I doing wrong?*

I've spent countless hours journalling, working with coaches, reading self-help books, listening to podcasts and doing personal development courses to try to resolve this issue. It wasn't until I started chatting more openly with friends and colleagues about *my* struggles with stress (which have led to burnout on more than one occasion) that I realised so many people are currently struggling with an increase in anxiety and overwhelm, and we're all saying the same things to ourselves. We've been suffering in silence – or worse, spending time looking for a new productivity system, app or tech tool to remedy the situation.

What if we've got it all backwards?

We think *we're* broken or inept. We question whether we're working hard enough, and we're struggling to stay on top of everything: the never-ending emails, WhatsApp and Teams messages, SMS notifications and news alerts, and our ever-growing to-do lists. In our quest to optimise our efficiency and master our time, we turn to tech tools and apps, but they only add to our digital overload.

We blame these perceived failings on a lack of organisation on our part, or a busy period at work, or a bulging inbox.

So many people are doing their best to conceal the fact that they're feeling this way. We keep pushing on in the hope that work will eventually slow down (spoiler alert: it won't), or we'll stop feeling overwhelmed when that big project is complete, or when we get promoted at work, or when we can finally catch up on some sleep. We delude ourselves with future visions of some sort of digital utopia where the Slack notifications stop pinging, the emails don't keep landing and the video calls are few and far between. But this digital utopia doesn't exist, and figure 0.3 illustrates why.

Figure 0.3: Our micro-stressors have increased, and our biological buffers have decreased

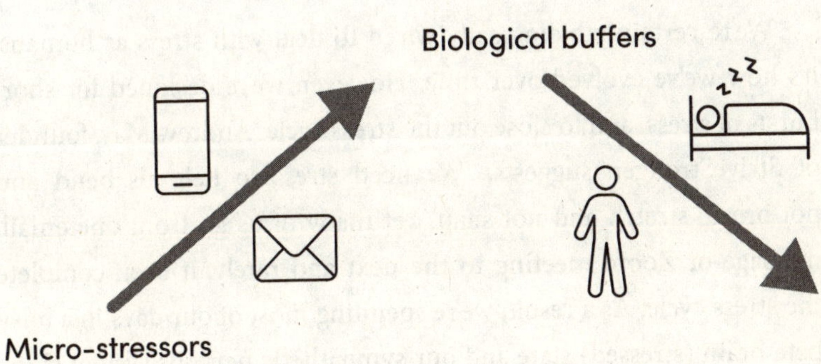

Our micro-stressors have increased

More and more people are indicating that they're stressed. In a 2021 survey conducted on behalf of the American Psychological Association, almost a third of respondents said that their stress levels were so high that they sometimes struggled to make basic decisions such as what to eat or wear. Obviously, there is some stress associated with living through a pandemic and global uncertainty, but there are other mechanisms at play that must be contributing to people feeling overwhelmed by day-to-day struggles. I think one of the chief culprits making us stressed is technology.

It's estimated that knowledge workers receive between 9000 and 15,000 emails per year, resulting in them spending around 16 per cent of their working time dealing with their inboxes. We've seen a 252 per cent increase in weekly video meeting times (no wonder so many of us suffer from Zoom fatigue), and we've started to work for longer stretches. Microsoft data suggests that knowledge workers' workdays have expanded by around 46 minutes each day – we're absorbing the commute with work. These behaviours are all micro-stressors. They may seem benign, and each on its own may in fact be harmless. However, they now permeate our days, and they accumulate over time.

We're certainly biologically wired to deal with stress as humans; it's how we've evolved over time. However, we're designed for short bursts of stress, and to close out the stress cycle. Andrew May, founder of StriveStronger, suggests, 'We need stress to help us bend and not break, stretch and not snap'. Yet many of us go from one email, message or Zoom meeting to the next and rarely, if ever, complete the stress cycle. As a result, we're spending most of our days in a busy beta brain (stressed) state and our sympathetic nervous system shifts us into a constant flight, fight or freeze mode to help us handle these micro-stressors.

Our biological buffers have been eroded

At the same time, our digital habits have also displaced some of the biological buffers that were once naturally baked into our days and helped us manage our stress. As a result, many of us feel OUSTED. Technology has altered our sleep, levels of physical movement, connections with others, stress tolerance, exposure to sunlight and even breathing.

A low-resolution version of yourself

In her book *Step Into You*, Lorraine Murphy suggests that people are living as 'low-res' versions of themselves. Many people are experiencing a sense of overwhelm, fatigue and distraction. Lisa Corduff, founder of The Change Room, conducted a study in 2022 with women across the globe and found that 63 per cent of women haven't felt full of energy for at least a year, and 38 per cent can't remember the last time they felt energised. They attributed their low energy to their mental load (75 per cent), stress or worry (71 per cent), lack of sleep (58 per cent) and spending too much time on their phones (45 per cent). Almost half of respondents (49 per cent) indicated that they were spending an average of three to four hours per day on screens on non-work-related activities (and 37 per cent spent one to two hours per day on this), with most indicating that they were spending this time on social media (77 per cent) and chats (7 per cent). We are really becoming slaves to our screens, and this is having a profound impact on our wellbeing.

Ask anyone today how they are and they'll likely answer with one of the two B's: 'busy' or 'burnt out'. In the 2021 Global Workplace Burnout Study, 34.7 per cent of people reported experiencing burnout symptoms. In a 2022 Microsoft report, 48 per cent of global employees and 53 per cent of global managers reported that they were experiencing burnout.

Let me be totally honest with you: I'm not immune to the digital pull. Despite researching, speaking and writing about digital burnout, I'm embarrassed to admit that I've had my experiences with burnout – times when I have pushed myself beyond the point of exhaustion. In fact, there were times when I was so exhausted that I had seizures. Along the way, I ticked all the boxes for burnout symptoms, but I chose to ignore them and kept pushing on until my body physiologically shut down.

Burnout led to me becoming a low-resolution version of myself. I was constantly exhausted, agitated and overwhelmed. I was brittle and frayed around the edges. No productivity system, no culling of my to-do list and no email management system could fix the problem – it was bigger than that. However, at the time, I couldn't see the wood from the trees. I was bogged in burnout.

As we experience burnout, our ability to handle additional stress reduces, and our cognitive and executive function can be compromised, along with a host of other serious physical and psychological consequences. I literally became oblivious to the fact that I was burnt out. My digital load increased exponentially, I started working in ways that were completely incongruent with my biology (even though I should have known better), and I felt trapped in the always-on, busy societal norm I'd bought into (and, I'm ashamed to say, I was perpetuating). The burnout symptoms were certainly there, but I chose to ignore them and push through.

Check to see if the World Health Organization's criteria for burnout are present in your own life:

- **Exhaustion:** Chronic sleep issues, digestive issues, a drop in libido, hair loss, and feeling short-tempered and teary over insignificant things are common symptoms of exhaustion. Burnout is characterised by physical and psychological depletion or exhaustion.

- **Cynicism:** Struggling to find your motivation, withdrawing from social activities, losing idealism, feeling irritable, feeling negative towards colleagues or clients, and feeling sceptical about your work can be red flags that cynicism has set in.
- **Reduced professional efficacy:** Has your productivity tanked? Do you feel less accomplished or capable than previously? Are you suffering from low morale and an inability to cope? These can all be signals of reduced efficacy.

(If you're curious about your actual risk of digital burnout, there is a free Digital Burnout Barometer assessment tool available in the 'Book Resources' section of my website.)

If you're struggling from burnout, or have previously, I want you to know that you're not broken or fundamentally flawed. You're not 'addicted'. You're not inefficient. And, no, you don't need a new productivity system or tech tool to remedy the situation!

You're not alone, and your burnout can be an opportunity for growth. Your agitated state can be an opportunity for you to find better, more sustainable ways of working and digital habits that are aligned with your neurobiology.

The solution isn't as simple as going on a #digitaldetox. (Spoiler alert: they don't work, because they don't result in long-term behavioural change.) It isn't to switch off completely for long periods of time because, let's face it, that doesn't last – and, for many of us, it isn't an option at all!

Instead, what we need to do is to find sustainable and healthy ways to integrate technology into our lives. We need to use our human operating system (hOS) to guide how we use technology.

As knowledge workers, we've been following a playbook that's outdated. Put simply, we've been working in ways that *don't* work for us. We need a new playbook that's based on the science of how our brains and bodies work best, and how they operate effectively in an online context. In her book *The Invisible Load*, Dr Libby Weaver suggests that we can turn down the volume on our overwhelm by better management of our digital devices. Now, as we are redefining our ways of working, is the chance for us to create ways of working that work for us as humans by aligning our digital behaviours to our hOS. We need to go back to our biology, look at what we humans need for optimal performance and map that to our digital ways of working and living.

It's time to find a digital operating system that leaves you feeling like a high-resolution version of yourself.

Upgrade your hOS

Burnout forced me to re-examine the ways in which I worked and question the world at large – why are we all buying into the 'busy' culture? Burnout was my soul screaming, 'Kristy, there's got to be a better way!' It was an invitation for me to evolve, adapt and change; it was an opportunity to work in a different way. I needed a different operating system. So I set out to test, refine and implement new ways of working based on how our brains and bodies work best online, on our hOS.

I've read, researched and (most importantly) applied a range of micro-habits to my life to tame my digital behaviours. I've made sure that the digital dimensions of my life work *with* my neurobiology, rather than *against* it – I've learned to control technology so it doesn't control me! I've put an end to feeling digitally distracted, dependent and disconnected. I've stopped feeling OUSTED.

Burnout was my catalyst for change, and significant change at that. I overhauled my unhealthy digital habits. I studied and implemented what our brains and bodies need for peak performance. And it changed my life.

We're at a critical juncture. As we redefine how, where and when we work in the wake of the pandemic, and as people are starting to examine the effects of the widespread adoption of digital technologies – for example, 'Facebook fatigue' – the time has come for us to examine critically our (sometimes complicated) relationships with technology.

While there's much conversation around 'flexible work arrangements' I believe the real opportunity lies in creating 'productive work arrangements', and the only way we can do this is by creating more sustainable digital habits that don't erode our wellbeing or dent our productivity. This is a paradigm-shifting moment, when we can structure our workdays to work *for* us and meet our neurobiological needs. It's time for us to abandon outdated modes of working, such as endless meetings, the normalisation of work on weekends or outside defined work hours, and constant multi-tasking.

Sure, we certainly can (and should, to some extent) blame the technology companies for their persuasive design techniques that got us (and our screenagers) hooked on our devices. However, we need to stop abdicating responsibility for our digital behaviours and instead focus on the things that we *can* do to tame our tech habits.

Instead, we need to cultivate digital practices that work *with* rather than *against* our brains and bodies. There are basic practices that we can implement to offset our digital demands.

We have an opportunity for us to better map our digital habits to our hOS. We must start to use digital technologies, both professionally and personally, to meet our most fundamental human needs. We are not machines. We cannot outperform our biological blueprint. We need to use our phones, laptops, tablets and other devices in ways that are congruent with our biology.

So, how can you upgrade your hOS? Don't fear, I won't propose that you cancel your Netflix subscription, aim for 'inbox zero' or go on a #digitaldetox. Instead, I'd like to empower you to put an end to feeling OUSTED and reverse the digital equation (as shown in figure 0.4).

Figure 0.4: Reduce your micro-stressors and increase your biological buffers

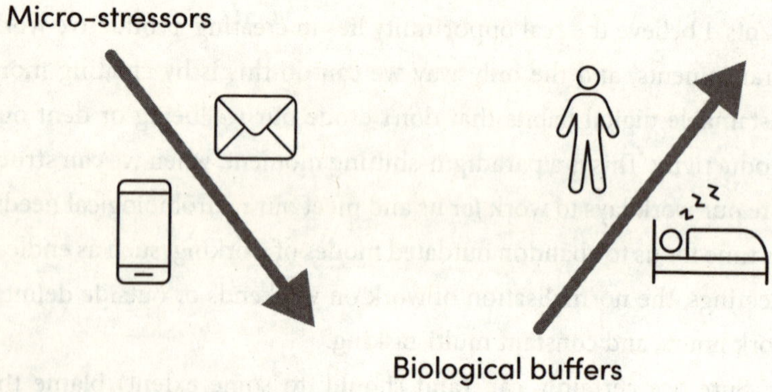

Reduce your micro-stressors

If we want to optimise our performance and protect our wellbeing in the digital world, we must reduce the micro-stressors that now permeate our days. While they may seem insignificant, and we don't typically stop to ponder how they're affecting us, micro-stressors can accumulate over time and impact us:

- **Alerts and notifications:** Alerts and notifications are some of the chief micro-stressors in our digitally dominated days. Our brains cannot differentiate between a tiger chasing us and a TikTok notification: both are perceived as a threat and subsequent stressor. Your brain sees the red notification bubble in your inbox declaring that you have 108 unread emails as a stressor – let's start by getting rid of that!

- **Work hours:** Research tells us that peak performance requires cycles of rest and recovery. We're biologically incapable of working for long stretches of time without periods of rest. Working longer hours doesn't lead to higher impact; in fact, working long hours can impair performance. The prefrontal cortex – the part of our brain that helps with problem-solving, complex thinking and working memory – is prone to fatigue. It only has a maximum battery life of approximately six hours per day (not 12 hours, as many of us try to do). We cannot expect that we can work for continuous stretches of time without adequate rest periods; that's working against our biology.
- **Working without breaks:** We need to create workplace cultures in which taking breaks is revered, not feared. Wellbeing isn't a set of slogans, a one-off lunch-and-learn workshop or token wellbeing days; it's best practices and norms informed by evidence and scientific rigour. Microsoft studies involving brain scans showed that stress levels drop dramatically if you simply take a ten-minute break between Teams meetings.
- **Zoom fatigue:** Videoconferencing closely resembles having a conversation with someone just 60 centimetres away from you. American anthropologist Edward Hall describes this distance as the 'intimate distance', typically reserved for telling secrets, cuddling, lovemaking, comforting, protecting, and playing football or wrestling. We reserve this distance for our loved ones or close friends… or, if really necessary, our enemies in a physical fight. It's the distance of mating or conflict – yet we're just on a Zoom call with Greg from accounts! Our brain can interpret this as a threat and, in turn, release cortisol (the stress hormone). There is a host of other reasons video calls are mentally fatiguing; I'll explain these in more detail later and, more importantly, arm you with brain-based strategies to tackle them.

- **Multi-tasking:** Multi-tasking, which has become a norm in our distributed workplaces, stresses the brain. Many of us now sit in Zoom meetings while also triaging our inboxes. When we multi-task, our brain burns through glucose – the brain's energy supply – and releases cortisol. Think of how frequently you multi-task, and consider the stress this is placing on your brain and body.
- **Always-on culture:** Our always-on culture has left many people feeling as if they can never switch off and take a psychological break from their work. The prevalence of communication tools such as Slack, Teams, WhatsApp and messages is causing 'availability creep' – the idea that many of us feel we need to be responsive at all hours. We need to establish digital guardrails – accepted digital norms, practices and principles that underpin how technology is used in organisations. How quickly does your team expect a Teams chat reply? Do you need to reply to your boss's emails at 11 p.m.?
- **Social stressors:** We're being exposed to more graphic content on a daily basis via social media and news sites. In years gone by, natural disasters, mass shootings and tragic accidents were certainly reported by the media, but these reports did not contain the raw video footage we now see that clearly shows horrific details. At best, in the past, a photo or written description of the incident was provided. Consuming a myriad of videos and social media posts about a tragic event is stressful – and this is how many of us start our days!

The good news is that there are digital habits that can eradicate many of the stressors that once derailed your day.

Increase your biological buffers

You cannot just reduce the micro-stressors in your life and expect that your stressful days will disappear – that won't be the case. In addition, you must fiercely protect some of the most basic biological needs that help you regulate your stress response.

When we work against our biology, it's like putting the wrong fuel in a Porsche and expecting it to go fast. What we need to do is prioritise the potent. We must embed the habits that help us manage stress (and also help us to focus):

- **Human connection:** One of our most fundamental needs is the need for relational connection. When we're with other people, we often laugh with them or imitate their mood and can co-regulate, thanks to our mirror neurons. (There's science to suggest that, yes, moods can be contagious.) Connecting with others, especially in person, can be an antidote to stress. When we're with other people, our brain releases oxytocin, which strengthens our bonds with others and reduces our stress and anxiety. Unfortunately, online interactions do not biochemically replicate in-person connections. In fact, research has shown that in-person interactions are far superior for reducing cortisol levels and enhancing oxytocin, compared with text-only and verbal-only interactions.
- **Sleep:** Research confirms that 20 per cent of Australians are woken up each night by alerts and notifications. Interrupted sleep means that people aren't completing their sleep cycles. A tired brain is ill-equipped to manage stress, because the prefrontal cortex doesn't work effectively; instead, the amygdala (the emotional hub of the brain) fires up. This is why we binge-watch TV, spend hours scrolling social media and make poorer food choices when we're tired. So, we need to protect the quantity and quality of our sleep.
- **Physical movement:** Humans are biologically designed to be active, not sit in front of a screen for hours at a time. Movement activates a range of neurotransmitters that make us feel good (such as dopamine, serotonin and noradrenaline) and help us to focus. Research also confirms that forward ambulation (for example, walking or running) activates dopamine and neuromodulators

that put the brain in an alert, focused state. Also, when we move, we create optic flow – this is the actual movement of objects passing us as we move, and it quietens the circuits that are responsible for stress. Have you ever found that you can solve a problem or feel far less stressed after a walk? Now you know why.

- **Sunlight:** Sunlight exposure can offset myopia (nearsightedness) and help reset our circadian rhythm, which supports sleep, and in doing so reduces stress, elevates mood and increases alertness. We need to ensure that our eyes are exposed to sunlight soon after waking (within 30 to 60 minutes is suggested); this controls the release of cortisol and melatonin, which impact sleep and mood. Sunlight also increases the brain's release of serotonin, a mood-boosting hormone that can help us feel calm and alert. While there aren't specific recommendations for adults, for children and teenagers at least 90 minutes of outdoor activity per day is advised.
- **Breathing:** We breathe differently when using devices. For example, we sigh significantly less when using screens. As mentioned earlier, sighing occurs roughly every five minutes and is our body's way of regulating the oxygen and carbon dioxide levels in our bodies. Sighing is a pattern of breathing that occurs spontaneously in sleep and when our carbon dioxide levels get too high, but we can also deliberately sigh to reduce our stress or anxiety levels quickly.
- **Stress tolerance:** Thanks to technological advancements, we rarely (if ever) feel cold or hot. As Paul Taylor explains in his book *Death by Comfort*, we live very comfortable lives thanks to our modern-day conveniences, such as air-conditioning and heating. Our bodies have become accustomed to being comfortable. But remember, our brains and bodies need stress; tolerable amounts of stress can nudge us to take action by heightening our focus and energy, and can be healthy for us.

Time to upgrade!

There are realistic, research-based actions we can take to ensure our digital behaviours don't erode or diminish our basic biological needs.

In the following sections of this book, I arm you with practices (and their accompanying micro-habits) that you can implement to ensure you reduce the micro-stressors in your life, and bolster the biological buffers that cushion you from stress so that you can flourish in this busy, always-on, digital world.

There are four pillars of digital peak performance that can help you thrive in the digital world, as shown in figure 0.5.

Figure 0.5: The four pillars of digital peak performance

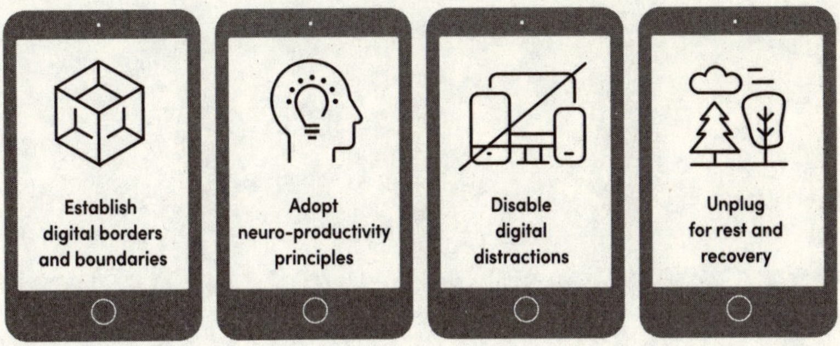

Each of the pillars contains three practices, and each practice involves three micro-habits that you can adopt to thrive in the digital age.

Making these small digital adjustments doesn't have to be complicated or convoluted. The basics work – if you work the basics. There are bedrock habits you can easily adopt that will transform your digital life and raise your stress threshold.

It's time for you to tame your tech habits and thrive in a distracted world.

PILLAR I

ESTABLISH DIGITAL BORDERS AND BOUNDARIES

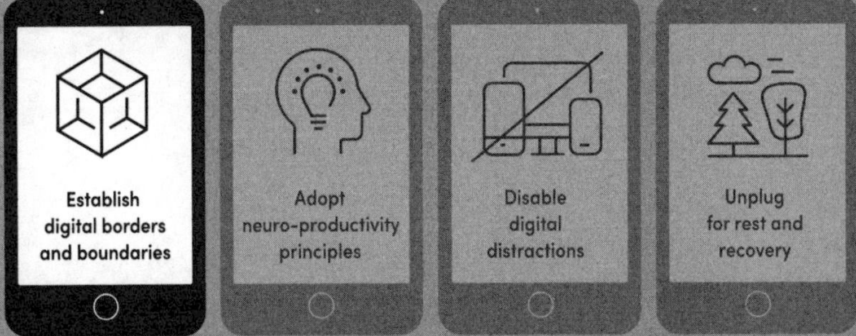

Me: Want to go for a walk on Sunday?

Kim: Love to. What time works best for you?

Kim: Hello?

Kim: Still want to meet for a walk?

Me: Sorry, I totally missed your replies. They got buried in the 16 other texts from the dentist, my electricity bill reminder and two-factor authentication messages from my bank.

Sound familiar? Our phones and devices have become sources of constant distraction and stress. We're being bombarded by constant messages, reminders, alerts and notifications. It's mentally taxing!

This is why we will first examine some of the most critical boundaries and borders we need to establish when using digital devices to support our physical health and mental wellbeing.

Pillar I comprises three key practices that will help you set your digital borders and boundaries:

1. Set your digital guardrails.
2. Boost your focus and reduce technostress.
3. Optimise your workspace.

Practice 1

Set your digital guardrails

Digital dementia. Nomophobia. Phantom vibration syndrome. Toilet tweeting. Yes, these are all real things! (Flick back to the preface for their definitions.)

Thanks to the omnipresence of mobile devices, technology has now infiltrated just about every facet of our lives and is having a profound impact on us. Therefore, we need to be intentional about how, where and when we use our devices. Creating cues, rituals and habits to encourage healthy digital behaviours is vital.

I've had the privilege of working with organisations, both large and small, to establish their digital guardrails: established and articulated norms, protocols, principles and practices around how digital technologies are used to facilitate hybrid work. These guardrails clearly delineate the ways in which teams want to use digital technologies by addressing many of the unspoken rules and expectations (or, as I refer to them, 'tech-spectations') around workplace technology behaviours.

Digital guardrails mean no more ambiguity around whether you need to have your camera turned on during a work Zoom call, how quickly you should expect a Teams chat reply, and how to communicate a critical or time-sensitive piece of information *without* sending an email and following it up with a Slack comment and then an SMS to check your colleagues received said email. (This is part of the 'Communication Escalation Plan', which provides one clear pathway for teams to communicate urgent matters – more often than not through a phone call.) Digital guardrails are a commonly accepted set of agreements about how your team can best use technology.

In the work I've done with multinational organisations and small businesses to establish their digital guardrails, I've found that success ultimately comes down to two things: constructing digital guardrails and leaders role-modelling the boundaries.

For example, a client I worked with, Nick, knew that his team felt like they were always on, and this was resulting in some members of his team teetering on the edge of digital burnout. Members of his team were frequently sending emails and Teams chats after 10 p.m. (This is not uncommon – Microsoft data has revealed that many teams are now seeing a 'triple productivity peak', with productivity bumping up at around 10 a.m., at 3 p.m. and again at 10 p.m., with 30 per cent of workers taking on a second shift after dinner.) He also had some team members report that they were chronically exhausted, and he overheard comments they made about feeling more negative towards their work. When Nick's team used my Digital Burnout Barometer assessment tool (which you can access on the Book Resources page of my website), they had, on average, a 'high' risk of digital burnout.

Nick's team and I worked together for three months to create his team's digital guardrails. When these digital guardrails were implemented across the team, Nick quickly observed some significant changes. His team were rarely sending emails late at night (or early in the morning, for that matter), they started to talk about their interests outside of work and they repeatedly mentioned that they weren't as tired as they previously had been. Data showed that their productivity had improved by 26 per cent and their stress levels had dropped by 43 per cent. Having clear digital parameters that were developed and accepted by the team and universally adopted (most of the time, at least) had a profound impact on all employees. They had found ways of working that worked for *them* and their organisation as well as their clients.

A study examining 40 universities in Australia shows why it's imperative that teams establish their digital guardrails: employees whose supervisors expected them to respond to work communications after hours reported higher levels of psychological distress (70.4 per cent compared with 45.2 per cent), emotional exhaustion (63.5 per cent compared with 35.2 per cent) and physical health symptoms such as headaches and back pain (22.1 per cent compared with 11.5 per cent) than those who did not. Responding to work communications outside of hours has implications on our ability to recover both physically and psychologically from work.

However, it's not just teams that need guardrails but also individuals. You need to establish your personal digital parameters. Your team may decide on a digital guardrail not to respond to emails outside defined work hours, but if your boss sends a barrage of emails at 3 p.m. on a Saturday and your colleagues start replying, while you know you don't *have* to reply, it's hard to avoid it when everyone else on your team is doing so.

This practice covers the three micro-habits that can help you set your tech boundaries.

Micro-habit 1: Establish your digital curfew

Sleep really is the elixir of life. Poor quality or quantity of sleep can have detrimental impacts on our physical health, mental wellbeing and performance. Our screen habits are among the chief culprits sabotaging our sleep. Therefore, it's paramount that you prioritise your sleep, and one of the best ways to do this is to establish your digital curfew.

Research conducted in 2021 found that 70 per cent of participants had experienced one or more sleep challenges since the start of the COVID-19 pandemic. Anecdotally, many of the corporate teams I worked with during the pandemic reported accumulating similar sleep durations as they'd had before the pandemic but feeling more fatigued. One plausible explanation for this 'tired and wired' feeling is that, during lockdown periods, many people were spending more time inside and online than they typically would have. In fact, research suggests that adults were spending an average of 13.28 hours per day on digital devices. As a result, many people were experiencing increased exposure to blue light emitted from their screens and weren't getting enough natural sunlight, especially within the first hour of waking up. Sunlight is required to reset our circadian rhythm. These factors may have hampered melatonin production, resulting in delayed onset of sleep and shorter sleep phases.

Have you ever noticed you tend to scroll social media more, binge-watch more Netflix, or are just generally more easily distracted when you're tired? You're not alone. The reason you succumb to your tech temptations when you're tired is because the part of your brain that helps to regulate your behaviour, your prefrontal cortex, doesn't work effectively when you're tired. Your brain knows that when you're tired, it must optimise its resources, so it will reduce the effectiveness of the frontal lobe to compensate for prioritising primary functions.

These digital distractions also give your brain quick dopamine hits, trapping you in a false cycle of digital appeal. This explains why we tend to make bad food choices when we're tired: it's simply that our prefrontal cortexes can't regulate our behaviour. This is also why many people succumb to 'revenge bedtime procrastination': the decision to delay sleeping at night and engage in monotonous socials scrolling or online shopping, often because of a perceived lack of free time earlier in the day.

Here are some of my favourite tips to create and stick to your digital curfew.

Set up a sleep reminder

Set up a reminder on your phone 90 minutes before you want to go to sleep so you can start to wind up your day. Over time, you will (hopefully) no longer rely on your phone to nudge you, because the habit will be entrenched.

Give yourself some digital-free time before bed

Switch off all digital devices ideally at least 60 minutes prior to sleep. If you're using digital devices – particularly small, handheld devices such as phones, tablets and laptops – in the 60 minutes before you sleep, you can adversely impact both the amount and quality of sleep you get each night. Digital devices emit blue light, which hits your pineal gland, which in turn inhibits the production of melatonin (the sleep hormone). Impaired melatonin production can delay the onset of sleep and reduce the deep and REM sleep stages, which are critical for memory consolidation.

Create a predictable wind-down ritual

A predictable wind-down ritual sends clear signals to your brain that the workday is done. This is particularly important when working from home, because simply seeing your laptop can be a cognitive trigger to think about work. Is it possible to put your laptop away, or close the door to your workspace?

Consider dimming the lights, having a bath or shower (elevating your body temperature can also aid your sleep), reading a book or magazine, or doing a mindfulness practice or some breathing exercises to put you in a relaxed state. Your brain has likely spent most of the day in a busy beta brain (stressed) state, so you need to find ways to unwind to help you get the restorative sleep that you need. Performing these activities has the added benefit of crowding out your evening tech time.

Do a screen swap before bed

Watching TV is a better choice at night than watching Netflix on your phone or laptop, because you tend to sit further away from the TV than smaller devices and therefore absorb less blue light. TV also tends to be more of a passive rather than interactive experience, so TV can be a calming pursuit (so long as what you're watching doesn't hyper-arouse you).

Establish a landing zone in your home

Having a designated spot where devices go at night to charge can help to keep devices out of bedrooms. Pop your device in the landing zone at least 60 minutes before you want to sleep. (See Practice 11 for more.)

Invest in blue-light-blocking glasses for use at night

If you really *must* be on your laptop at night – I get it, sometimes there's a deadline or critical work incident you need to deal with – consider wearing blue-light-blocking glasses to help reduce blue light exposure. I personally use and recommend Baxter Blue glasses (see the Book Resources page of my website for a special discount code). They will have their most potent impact if worn from around 4 p.m. into the evening.

Dim the brightness

In the evening, we really need to reduce all blue-light exposure, not just that coming from our screens. Fluorescent and energy-efficient lights can all emit blue light, so consider dimming the lights in your house, or using candles or lamps at night. Close any curtains to reduce external light sources.

Micro-habit 2: Identify your no-go tech-zones

Which are the places and spaces in your home where you're happy for technology to enter, and which are the sacred spaces that you want to keep tech-free? You need to identify the no-go tech-zones in your home; ideally, bedrooms, bathrooms, meal areas and cars should be as screen-free as possible.

You don't want to bookend your day with your phone. If your phone travels into your bedroom, you're much more likely to reach for it first thing in the morning and last thing at night. Scrolling on your device in the morning or at night impacts your stress response: it activates your limbic system, which is your body's primitive (but very effective) threat alert system. The fight, flight or freeze response begins in the limbic system.

When you experience a stressful event – which your brain may perceive checking your inbox or reading colleagues' LinkedIn updates to be – the amygdala, an area of the brain that helps with emotional processing, sends a distress signal to the hypothalamus. This part of the brain functions like a command centre: it communicates with the rest of your body through the nervous system. This stress response activates the sympathetic nervous system so you have the energy to fight or flee.

Scrolling through your phone or opening the laptop lid first thing in the morning, especially when you're coming out of a beautiful, restful state, can really jolt your brain and cause you to feel unnecessarily stressed. When you wake, you transition into a delightful theta brain state (theta brain waves help us to process information and make memories), so you really want to protect that time and not erode it.

Having your phone or laptop in your room at night can adversely impact the quality and quantity of your sleep. You want your brain to associate the bedroom with the two S's: sex and sleep, *not* screens. Research tells us that 20 per cent of Australian adults are woken each night because of alerts and notifications. These digital disruptions interfere with your sleep cycle: when you fall back to sleep, you start your sleep cycle again, rather than picking up where you left off. So, many people are not getting enough completed sleep cycles because they're being woken up by their phones. Adults need four to six completed sleep cycles each night and many people are not meeting this quota.

Even if it's not alerts waking you up, just seeing your phone when you naturally wake up to go to the bathroom or get a glass of water can be enough of a psychological trigger to think about issues that may worry you. For example, you roll over, see your phone and start wondering if your tricky client responded to your email, or if your boss has sent you yet another late-night tirade of emails. These thoughts can obviously hyper-arouse your brain and make it challenging to fall back to sleep.

So, what do we do?

Get an alarm clock

I know, many of you will tell me your phone is your alarm clock. Could you invest in an old-fashioned alarm clock to keep digital devices outside of your bedroom? This is one of the inclusions in the Digital Wellbeing Boxes I send to clients.

Use a phone storage box

If you (or your screenagers) really lack the self-control to keep devices out of your bedroom, consider a lockable box such as those from inchargebox. One of the simplest yet most effective inventions I've seen, developed by a mum of screenagers, is a stylish, steel, lockable box that can charge up to 12 devices at once, including iPhones, iPads, PS4 gaming controllers and 13-inch laptops. You can pop it on the kitchen bench, in the office, or anywhere you'd like to lock and charge your devices. (I personally use these with my family, so I've secured a promo code you can find on the Book Resources page of my website.)

Put it on silent and out of sight

If your phone really *must* come into your bedroom at night, ensure it is on aeroplane mode and it is out of sight: hide it in a drawer, or pop a book on top of it. Just seeing it can be a psychological trigger for you to think about work.

Have a digital depot for mealtimes

If you want to keep devices away from set areas in your house, such as the meal area, establish a designated spot where phones go at set times. This ensures that there's no ambiguity about where devices go. You could even encourage your dinner guests to do the same thing, too, to stop them from 'phubbing' (phone snubbing).

Activate driving mode

Fatal car accidents from distracted drivers have increased over recent years. It's now common to see people sitting at traffic lights looking at their phone (or, worse still, while they're driving). To help you stay focused on driving, you can now automatically activate 'driving mode' when your car picks up your phone's bluetooth connection. You can customise your driving settings and even set automated replies to messages. This can help to manage other people's tech-spectations and can have a positive contagion effect, too: I've had numerous replies from people who've messaged me while driving and received my automated reply asking me how to set it up!

Micro-habit 3: Rest your eyes

Many people report experiencing digital eye strain from spending hours each day staring at a screen for professional and personal reasons. Prolonged periods of time in front of screens can result in headaches, blurred vision, tired eyes, red eyes and neck aches.

Below are some tips to help you rest your eyes.

Follow the 20-20-20-20 rule

To help prevent the symptoms associated with digital eye strain, optometrist Karen Garner-Hamilton suggests that people follow the 20-20-20-20 rule: for every 20 minutes you're using a screen, take at least a 20 second break, look at something 20 feet (around 6 metres) away to change your depth of vision, and blink 20 times. The reason our eyes are often tired after a long day in front of a screen is that our blink rate drops by around 66 per cent. Blinking keeps the cornea lubricated, removes debris and brings nutrients, minerals and other beneficial substances to the surface of the eye.

The elbow rule

Karen also suggests using the elbow rule to determine the working distance at which near work should be performed, as it's an easy way to remember: placing your hand on your chin, your screen should be no closer than your elbow.

Hook this habit onto other habits

When you go to the bathroom, make a cup of tea or look away from your computer monitor while thinking, implement this strategy. Attaching new habits to existing habits can be a great way to make new habits stick, according to James Clear in his book *Atomic Habits*.

Dilate your gaze throughout the day

Your eyes need regular screen breaks throughout the day. Going from back-to-back Zoom meetings to then 'take a break' by checking emails on your phone is *not* an ideal strategy. When you have a break, try to dilate your gaze to create divergence in your eyes. This will help your eyes and your body to relax. Perhaps go outside and look at the sky, or go for a quick walk near the beach or at the local park. Even just looking out the window can help, because a dilated gaze activates your parasympathetic nervous system and helps you to feel relaxed.

Spending hours looking at your devices creates convergent movement, which elevates your stress response. This can be traced back to our evolution: we adopt a narrow field of focus when we're in a heightened, stressed state so we can laser in on the perceived threat. The problem is that, nowadays, we spend the preponderance of our days with a narrow field of focus as we stare at our laptops and desktops, and this elevates our stress levels.

Close your eyes throughout the day

Working online all day is mentally depleting. Stanford University researchers (among others) have suggested that Zoom fatigue – the colloquial expression to explain any sort of cognitive fatigue that results from video meetings – is a real scientific phenomenon. The temporal and occipital lobes in the brain, which process what we hear and see online, are working overtime on video calls. Another part of the brain called the 'fusiform gyrus', which processes faces, is highly active on video calls, as it's processing the Brady Bunch–style layout of faces. This is why we easily fatigue from virtual or hybrid meetings.

A simple technique to counter this video fatigue is to simply close your eyes for 30 seconds. This gives your occipital lobe and fusiform gyrus a much needed rest and reboot. It moves your brain from a busy beta state into an alpha brain state, where you're focused and alert. Best of all, you can apply this strategy during your virtual calls when you feel the fatigue set in. The trick is to sit very still and mute yourself, and you can simply pretend that your camera froze!

Shrink the size of your meeting windows

Another technique is to shrink the size of the Zoom window and sit further away from your monitor. Most of us sit around 60 centimetres from our computer monitor and, depending on the size of your computer screen and the number of participants on the video call, the heads can sometimes appear very close to you. Remember, this space is typically reserved for what's referred to as 'intimate distance', which our brain associates with stress and awkwardness.

Summary

1. Establish your digital curfew.
2. Identify your no-go tech-zones.
3. Rest your eyes.

Practice 2

Boost your focus and reduce technostress

Today, stress can seem unrelenting. You unlock your phone and there's a message reminding you your gas bill is overdue. There's an uptick in your cortisol level. You open your inbox and there's a complicated client email that elicits a stress response. There's an uptick in your cortisol level. You don't have time to respond because your calendar is telling you there's a Teams meeting looming in five minutes, and you haven't had time to read the notes required before the meeting, so there's another cortisol uptick. You finish your meeting and jump back into your inbox to reply to the tricky client email, and there are 15 more emails that you need to attend to, so there's another cortisol uptick.

Our days are now dominated by digital stressors that rarely end. We rarely, if ever, feel like we've closed the stress cycle. We no longer have short periods of stress. Our days are punctuated by constant micro-stressors.

Your brain is continuously scanning the physical environment for sensory data. It is estimated that the body sends the brain around 11 million pieces of sensory data per second (10 million of which come from the eyes), but your conscious mind is capable of processing between 40 and 50 pieces per second. Your brain likes to form shortcuts, so it creates neural pathways based on the sensory data you receive. For example, smelling coffee or seeing your desk at work might be cognitive triggers you've associated with work. This is why many people found working remotely so challenging at first: the bedroom, a place associated with rest and relaxation, suddenly became the boardroom. Dr Sahar Yousef and Professor Lucas Miller from Becoming Superhuman refer to these as 'muddled associations'.

The problem arises when your brain cannot predict what associations to form when seeing a sensory cue. This is exactly what happens with your digital devices: you see your phone or laptop and your brain cannot predict what neural pathways to activate. Will you turn on your phone to be greeted by a cacophony of voicemail pings, SMS notifications and email alerts? Will these notifications bear good or bad news? (Negativity bias means many of us assume that it will be the latter.)

Research has even shown that some people suffer from email apnoea (or 'screen apnoea'). Linda Stone coined the term in 2008 to describe the common phenomenon of unconsciously holding one's breath, or breathing shallowly, when responding to emails or while texting. Your pupils dilate and your heart rate accelerates, all in response to your emails! Stone suggested that up to 80 per cent of people may experience this phenomenon. When you're stressed or focused, your brain knows that it needs to prioritise resources (brainpower) for the task at hand, so it switches off certain subconscious activities, such as breathing and hunger (ever noticed you often don't feel hungry when you're stressed?). You temporarily inhibit some subconscious brain activities to divert resources to perform the difficult task.

Holding your breath contributes to a range of stress-related diseases and can also disrupt the body's balance of oxygen, carbon dioxide and nitric oxide levels, which are necessary to fight infection and manage inflammation in the body. Changes in your breathing can trigger the sympathetic nervous system's fight, flight or freeze response, impacting your health, wellbeing and capacity to work productively. If your brain perceives a threat – and remember, your brain sees emails in the same way it would see a tiger approaching – it prioritises resources for your survival and away from the prefrontal cortex (the thinking part of the brain). If you stay stuck in this perceived state of emergency – this state of hyper-arousal – for prolonged periods of time, it can adversely impact your sleep, learning and memory, and can possibly exacerbate anxiety and depression.

Of course, no-one wants to hold their breath every time they open an email, so let's look at three micro-habits to focus on to manage technostress and boost focus.

Micro-habit 1: Increase your green time to balance your screen time

We've shifted far from our biological roots. We once spent most of our days outdoors but, today, most adults – and children and teens, I dare say – spend the bulk of their waking hours indoors (and sedentary). Humans are biologically designed to be in natural environments; we're not designed to spend hours inside hunched over a small screen.

Whether it's a stroll through your local park or a trek through a rainforest, time in nature – colloquially referred to as 'green time' – has been shown to have a myriad of benefits, such as reducing stress and bolstering focus. It's the balm for our busy brains, because it's naturally slower paced than our frantic digital world. It has become a widely accepted practice, with some people even engaging in 'forest bathing' – intentionally spending time in nature for restorative benefits.

Researchers have provided various scientific explanations for the benefits of green time. The biophilia hypothesis suggests that, because our ancestors evolved in wild settings and relied on nature for their survival, we have an innate drive to connect with nature. The stress reduction theory proposes that spending time in natural settings triggers a physiological response that lowers stress. Finally, the attention restoration theory posits that nature replenishes our cognitive resources, which in turn restores our ability to focus and pay attention (a skill that's seriously under threat, as this book explores in Pillar III).

It's highly plausible that time in nature is beneficial due to a combination of all three factors, as we know there's a symbiotic relationship between stress and attention. Put simply, a stressed brain finds it challenging to focus. Nature will nurture you.

So, how much green time do you need? A 2019 study found that spending between 20 and 30 minutes strolling through or sitting in a place that makes you feel in contact with nature will significantly reduce your cortisol levels. Another study suggests that even 40 seconds can be sufficient to reduce cortisol levels.

Exposure to sunlight, which occurs when we're in nature, has also been shown to be a fundamental biological need that's shifted in recent years. Increased time on devices, coupled with a global trend for urbanisation, means that people are increasingly experiencing less natural sunlight each day. Sunlight is critical for establishing our circadian rhythm, which help us with sleep and has been shown to boost our mood, improve our focus and help offset myopic progression (nearsightedness).

So, here are my tech-tips for getting more green time.

Shift some of your virtual meetings to walking meetings

You obviously can't do this for all meetings but, when possible, pop your earbuds in and take a walk around your local park while doing your Zoom or Teams call. Determine in advance if it will be an audio-only call and, if not, ask if you could attend in audio-only format. This is contingent upon the type of meeting, the complexity of issues that need to be discussed and whether you need to refer to or take notes.

I've found that when you're direct about why you want to have your camera off, people are much more receptive to the idea. It often has a contagion effect: others will emulate your behaviour and switch some of their meetings to virtual walking meetings.

Aim to get 20 to 30 minutes of natural sunlight within the first hour of waking up

Viewing sunlight by going outside within 30 to 60 minutes of waking up is one of the best things you can do for your physical and mental health, according to Professor Andrew Huberman. Sunlight exposure in the morning promotes the healthy functioning of your hormone system. Photosensitive cells in your eyes impact your brain's hypothalamus region, which in turn controls your biological clock. Morning light triggers the activation of cortisol, which puts your body into a state of focus and alert; it also sets off a timer of about 16 hours to peak melatonin levels to help you sleep.

Two minutes of morning sunlight is a minimum, ten minutes is great, and thirty minutes is fabulous. The photons will still cut through the clouds on an overcast day, so you should try to do this daily. If you wake up while it's dark, turn on all the lights in your house and go outside once the sun has risen. Yes, you can get sunlight sitting in your car or through a window in your kitchen, but it's 50 per cent less effective through a window, because the glass filters out wavelengths that are essential for stimulating the eyes and sending the wake-up signal to your brain.

You should never look directly at the sun. Aim to have sunlight exposure without sunglasses.

Aim to get 90 minutes of sunlight each day

Sunlight is vital for our most basic biological functions, and for our psychological and physical health.

As mentioned earlier, research tells us that sunlight exposure can help offset myopia (nearsightedness), although it's uncertain at this stage what mechanism is at play here. Is it that when you're outside, direct sunlight on your skin causes your body to create vitamin D, which could act as a protective factor reducing the impact of near focus elongating the eye? Or is it that when you're outside, you naturally broaden your gaze as you watch that bird in the distance or track the ball that's flying towards you?

Your biological need for sunlight is dependent on your skin tone, age (you generally need more sunlight as you age, because your eyes are less able to take in light), health, diet and where you live. As a baseline, 10 to 20 minutes during the summer and spring months is sufficient, and usually two hours in winter and autumn (and always use the necessary sun protection when required).

Get some afternoon light

As the sun is setting, try to spend a couple of minutes outside when you can. According to Professor Andrew Huberman, this sends a powerful signal to your brain that the day is ending and sets off powerful hormonal cascades that will set your body up for sleep later in the evening.

Micro-habit 2: Take micro-movement breaks

Have you ever felt stressed, then taken a walk and felt like your stress has dissipated? Or perhaps you've taken a walk and a genius idea has germinated, or you've solved a complex problem you've spent months agonising over.

Movement is a fabulous tool we can use to manage our stress. However, today we're spending less time being physically active and much more time being sedentary, thanks to our plugged-in lifestyles.

A brief hiatus from your desk enables you to disengage from work and has been shown to reduce stress, improve focus and have a calming restorative effect. Micro-movement breaks help counter the ill effects of sitting at your desk for too long, which we know is particularly detrimental to our physical health.

As humans, one of our most fundamental biological needs is movement. When we move, we create optic flow, whereby visual images pass by our eyes. Neuroscience confirms that, when we walk, the optic flow decreases activity in the amygdala, which is the part of the brain responsible for fear and anxiety. When this region of the brain isn't active, we can think more creatively and clearly.

Aerobic exercise – such as walking, running and cycling – can also give the brain a bubble bath of neurochemicals such as dopamine, serotonin, noradrenaline and brain-derived neurotrophic factor (BDNF), which give the hippocampus (important for learning and memory) a boost. When we're stressed or anxious, we don't remember much because our neural activity is concentrated in the amygdala and not as much in the hippocampus.

So, here are some ways you can prioritise your micro-movement breaks.

Walk-and-talk meetings

It's not just your virtual meetings that you should change to walking meetings if you can, but also your in-person meetings. Some studies show that walking meetings can increase creative thinking by up to 60 per cent. Steve Jobs reportedly held many walking meetings.

The trick is to include some buffer time at the end of the walk to document all that you talked about. Be prepared: there may be a lot to record as the ideas flow when you walk.

Set a timer

Set a timer in your calendar to help you be more intentional about taking regular micro-movement breaks.

Keep some prompts nearby

In his book *Atomic Habits*, James Clear suggests that to embed new habits, you need to use cues that will trigger the desired behaviour. For example, if you see some exercise bands next to your workstation, or your sneakers under your desk, you're more likely to use them.

Compile a micro-movement list

Reduce any decision fatigue by keeping a list of micro-movement breaks you enjoy near your workstation. If you enjoy them, you're more likely to do them more frequently. Seeing the list may also nudge you (pardon the pun) to get up from your desk and move.

Micro-habit 3: Breathe better

Breathing is one of the most effective tools we have at our disposal to beat stress. It's free, accessible at any time and doesn't require us to step away from the stressful event or situation, unlike other stress-combatting tools such as mindfulness, meditation or massage. We can discreetly implement this strategy even while sitting in a stressful Teams meeting or tackling our inboxes.

Research confirms that the physiological sigh can help you regulate your stress response. As explained in the introduction to this book, a physiological sigh is a pattern of breathing that involves two inhales and an exhale. Humans naturally sigh every five minutes to regulate oxygen and carbon dioxide levels. Sighing sends a message to your nervous system that you're safe, so it can take you from a stressed sympathetic-nervous-system state and instead activate the parasympathetic nervous system.

However, recent research tells us that our sigh rate drops when using digital devices. This indicates that we're in a heightened state of stress when using our screens. We may notice this by observing our shallow breathing.

So, here are some tips to help you breathe better.

Use the physiological sigh when you're feeling stressed

It's easy to sigh when you're stressed. Do a longer first inhale through the nose, a second smaller inhale through the nose and then an exhale through the mouth. This allows you to offload carbon dioxide and take in more oxygen. One to three sighs are enough to reduce your stress response.

Make your exhalations longer than your inhalations

One of the quickest ways to manage stress is to do some deep breathing. Science has shown that taking control of your breathing can change the firing of your locus coeruleus, which impacts your production of noradrenaline (which makes you feel stressed).

There is a myriad of deep breathing techniques, from box breathing to diaphragmatic breathing, alternate nostril breathing to 4-7-8 breathing (where you breathe in for a count of four, hold for a count of seven and then breathe out for a count of eight). So long as you exhale for longer than you inhale, breathing will have a calming impact: it will stimulate your vagus nerve, which will lower your heart rate and activate the parasympathetic nervous state (your rest-and-digest state). According to Sophie Scott, an Adjunct Associate Professor at the University of Notre Dame's medical school, the vagus nerve is a fundamental part of the parasympathetic nervous system (which returns your body to a normal state after a fight, flight or freeze response), so vagus nerve stimulation can have a huge impact on your mental health.

Set a reminder on your phone's lock screen

While you try to embed these new habits, the use of reminders will encourage you to make these behaviours habitual. Given that the average adult picks up their phone 96 times per day, seeing a reminder on your lock screen might give you a nudge to breathe.

Note that while some people find that a calendar reminder to breathe every hour can be helpful, others find it even more stressful, because it's yet another interruption and micro-stressor that intrudes their day.

Summary

1. Increase your green time to balance your screen time.
2. Take micro-movement breaks.
3. Breathe better.

Practice 3

Optimise your workspace

The absence of a commute and having fewer distractions while we work are among the top reasons people like working remotely. Let's not forget that working from home means we can now avoid listening to Simon loudly recount his weekend shenanigans at the water cooler, or hearing Rebecca slurp her way through her green smoothie every morning at 8.30.

At the time of writing, over 70 per cent of employees have indicated that they want to work remotely at least two or three days per week and, if this isn't offered, more than half of employees say they'll look elsewhere for employment that does offer this flexibility.

The problem is that not everyone has a designated workspace at home. In a 2022 PwC study, 79 per cent of people who had a dedicated workspace at home reported that their mental health and wellbeing improved when working remotely; the figure wasn't as high for those who didn't have a specific work location at home. It appears that there is a tangible cost of working at the kitchen bench. During the COVID-19 pandemic, social media was awash with photos of people's makeshift office set-ups, with people perching laptops on upturned laundry baskets, converting kitchen tables to boardrooms and even one tall guy putting his laptop on top of his fridge.

Even if you're lucky enough to have a study nook or home office, it might have its problems. You might still have your neighbour start their lawnmower at the precise time your important Teams call starts; or perhaps your partner is sharing your workspace and you can't focus on your work when you discover they're *that* person at work who says, 'I'll circle back to you'.

Our physical environment has a significant impact on our mood, our productivity, our physical health and even our thinking. The way we structure our day also has an impact on how we perform.

So, let's look at how to best structure your physical workspace – whether you're in the office, working remotely or choosing to work from a café or shared workspace – and the three micro-habits that will enhance how you work in a digitally saturated context.

Micro-habit 1: Sit-stand-switch

Humans are spending more time sitting down than they ever have in history. Today, many of us perform desk jobs, travel in vehicles and dedicate hours of our leisure time to our phones and laptops. It is estimated that the average knowledge worker spends more than nine hours each day sitting, both at work and home. This is completely different to how our ancestors spent their days and contravenes one of the chief requirements of our biological blueprint: movement.

Sedentary behaviour is linked to a range of adverse physical health conditions, such as diabetes, cardiovascular disease and some cancers. People who sit for long periods have been found to have higher rates of mental health issues, too, such as depression (although it can sometimes be difficult to separate cause and effect). This was originally thought to be because people were more likely to be obese, but there's now evidence that even if you're not overweight, sedentary behaviour can still put you at greater risk of these health issues.

While you may think that the solution is simply to go and buy a standing or walking desk, that won't solve the problem. There are two issues at play in our modern world dominated by digital devices:

1. We're sitting for long durations throughout the day.
2. We're not frequently breaking up periods of sitting with other incidental movement like we used to do.

While a standing desk might solve the first issue, it doesn't address the second issue. Also, the problem with standing or walking desks is that many people adopt unhealthy postures as they fatigue while using them, which can cause further ailments.

During the shift to remote work, many people observed that their step count was down; this is because they lost a lot of the incidental movement they used to do, even when working in an office. They used to walk to the printer, walk to the local café for their morning coffee and walk (or run, if late) to the bus stop; all of this was quickly eradicated as they started working from their kitchen benches. For many people, the map shown in figure 3.1, overleaf, is what their physical movement patterns looked like while working from home.

Recent research shows that even if you're meeting the suggested guidelines for physical movement each day (150 minutes of moderate-intensity exercise per week), the benefits are largely nullified if you're sitting for more than five hours per day. Let's face it, many of us are now sedentary for more than five hours per day. Those people who are diligent about their F45 or gym workouts yet sit down in front of their computer for hours each day and barely move (apart from occasional tea and wee breaks) could be jeopardising their health, simply because they're spending too much time sitting down.

Prolonged time sitting hunched over devices can also cause a range of musculoskeletal problems. Many of us have developed tech neck, which is the colloquial term used to describe the aches and pains caused by spending hours hunched in front of screens. If you regularly sit at a desk, you've probably experienced neck ache, back pain or shoulder stiffness at some point; this is due to incorrect ergonomic set-ups, coupled with prolonged periods of inactivity. The more we fatigue, the unhealthier our postures tend to become. After a long day in front of my laptop, I find myself with my legs tucked up on my chair and I'm stooping down to look at my screen.

Figure 3.1: Your work-from-home movement patterns?

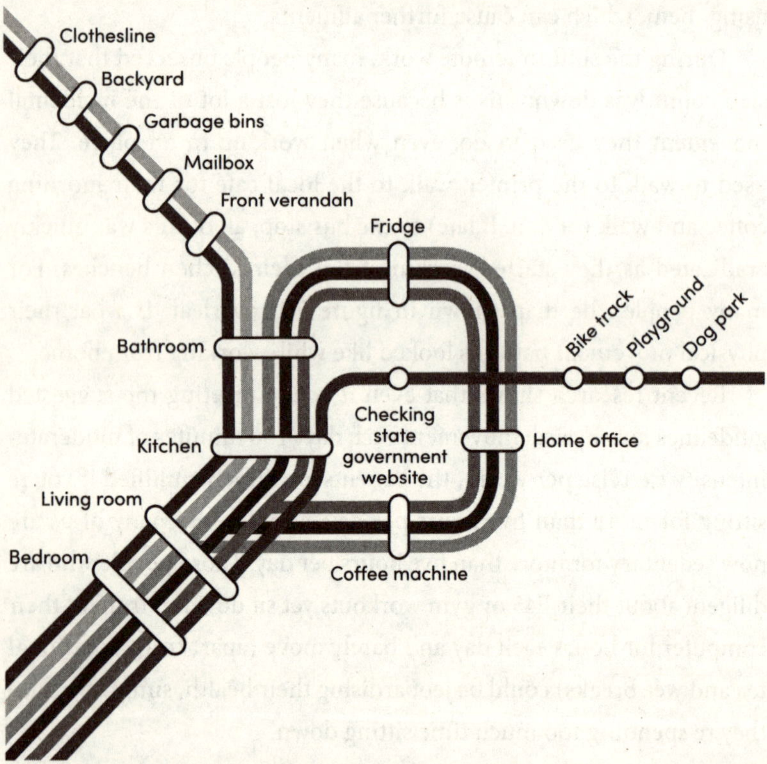

Here are some tech-tips to get you moving more.

Set a 1:1 ratio for sitting and standing

Alternate between sitting and standing in a 1:1 ratio. So, if you sit for an hour, try to stand for an hour (or thereabouts).

Set a timer

To nudge you to revert from sitting to standing, set a timer on your laptop or phone to remind you to reposition yourself throughout your workday. It doesn't need to be precise, so long as you do it frequently throughout the day and avoid any long bouts of sitting.

Invest in a stand-up desk (or make your own)

There is an array of stand-up desks that you could purchase (or, if you're lucky, your organisation might purchase one for you). Alternatively, create a stand-up desk using a box or a pile of books.

Plan three or four ten-minute walks each day

Have you ever come back from a walk and felt *worse* than when you left? Me neither. Movement interspersed throughout your day will provide physical benefits, boost your mood and even bolster your performance. Professor Huberman suggests that three or four ten-minute walks scattered throughout your day are enough to counter sitting for more than five hours per day.

Stand up for your phone calls

Standing up for your phone calls could dramatically increase the time you spend standing if you make a lot of calls.

Stand-up meetings

If you have an in-person meeting, suggest that you spend the first ten minutes standing. You can then revert to sitting, if preferred. You may be surprised – people may choose to stand for longer.

Engage in a step challenge

During the pandemic, many teams engaged in step challenges to create team cohesion and encourage team members to improve their step counts, which many noticed had nosedived since working remotely. People love a bit of healthy competition, and a step challenge is a great way to foster this and boost team members' physical health and productivity at the same time.

Micro-habit 2: Set it up right

Whether you're in the office or working from home, the set-up of your physical space is critical to optimise your performance. When you better understand your brain and body's biological needs, you can better organise your physical space. When you set up your workstation the right way, you can stop fatigue from setting in and bolster your focus.

Here are some simple but effective ways of setting up a better workspace.

Light it up in the day

During the daytime, you want light to come from above you. Overhead lights hit the neurons in your eyes that send a message to your hypothalamus to create a state of alertness. Light stimulates the production of dopamine, epinephrine (also known as adrenaline) and cortisol, which put you in a state of high alert. A bright workspace is ideal for deep, focused work.

Dim it down in the late afternoon and night

From around 4 p.m. onwards (or typically nine hours after waking up, whenever that is), you want light to come from the side or below. Use a desk lamp or ring light during these times.

Set it up

Ideally, you want your screen height at or above your nose level. We instinctively know this, as we hunch over to accommodate a low desk. The trick is to adjust your desk – perhaps pop a pile of books under your laptop, or use a desk elevator – and not move your body to the screen.

Professor Andrew Huberman says it's important that you glance slightly up when working on your screen (you don't want to bend your neck at all), as this keeps the neurons in your eyes active, which triggers brain circuits associated with alertness. When we look down, in comparison, it creates neurons that are calming and sleep-inducing. This is why many people look down when they're meditating, doing a mindfulness practice or praying.

Location, location, location

Have you ever sat in the foyer of a hotel and had really creative ideas, or come up with a genius solution to a problem? Research has shown that there's a relationship between the height of the ceiling and the types of cognition that follow: the higher the ceiling, the loftier the ideas you'll have. Lower ceilings tend to instigate feelings of confinement, while high ceilings inspire you and give you a sense of freedom. It's called the 'cathedral effect'.

So, when you want to brainstorm some new ideas for a project, or think in a creative or abstract way, try to find a location with a high ceiling.

Work in places with lower ceilings when you need to undertake more concrete or detail-oriented thinking. This is another benefit of hybrid work: you can now work in different locations to elicit different types of thinking. Don't have a room with a low ceiling? In the *Huberman Lab* podcast, Huberman suggests you wear a brimmed hat or hoodie when you need to do analytic, detail-oriented work;

this limits your field of vision to help you focus on the task at hand by removing some of the visual distractions that may divert your attention.

Limit your view

If you want to engage in focused work, try to eliminate as many distractions in your visual field as possible. Your cognition is significantly influenced by the visual data you process; remember, your eyes are receiving around 10 million pieces of sensory data per second. If you want to focus, limit what comes into your line of sight. Create some barriers around your visual field, as this will limit distractions and meet your brain's need for safety. (As the descendants of cave dwellers, we feel safe in small spaces.)

If working in an open-plan office, or in a large room at home, create some barriers around your workstation. This will create a sense of safety, even in an open space. For example, could you select a seat next to a wall, use bookshelves or room dividers, or even put your back to the open area? If working at home, could you position your desk so you're looking at a wall or a space with few visual distractions?

Have designated spots

Regardless of where you work, it's important that you perform similar types of work tasks in the same location, because this will help you retain information. It's referred to as 'state-dependent memory'. Could you do your deep, focused work in your study nook and clear your inbox on your balcony?

Personalise your space

One of our most basic psychological needs as humans is safety. Adding personal artefacts to your workspace that are meaningful to you can help you feel secure and safe. Now's your chance to put up your *Flintstones* figurines or other strange artefacts that you love but would never dare take to work. Could you add some family photos or objects that have sentimental value?

Eliminate background noise

Of the 11 million pieces of sensory data your brain is receiving every second, it needs to decipher what to process and what to disregard. While your brain is effective at extracting important information you need and ignoring the rest, this comes at a cost: it takes a significant amount of energy to filter out superfluous information, especially background speech or noises. This is why it's important to eliminate as much background noise as possible. (Later, I explain the benefits of wearing noise-cancelling headphones when working in a noisy office, or working remotely with a noisy partner or flatmate.)

Melissa Marsden, Workplace Strategist and Founder of COMUNiTI explains:

> 'The design, layout and proximity of space in our workplaces has a significant impact on our productivity and performance. When we fail to consider the use of our spaces and the relationship of one space to another, we are contributing to the effects of increased levels of noise and distraction, which research has shown reduces our psychological wellbeing and therefore our experience and performance at work.
>
> 'Take, for example, a "quiet space" positioned directly adjacent the staff kitchen – seems obvious, but it happens a lot. This relationship of spaces contradicts the intended use of each space, with the quiet room unable to perform its role in supporting quiet and concentrative work due to the poor acoustic separation, directly impacting on the ability of our people to perform to their desired level.'

Work in a café

Many people find they are productive when working in a café. Yet cafés are typically noisy places. However, this is white noise. It activates what's called the 'cocktail party effect', which refers to our selective attention. In an environment rich with sounds, we need to tune into salient information and tune out background noise or chatter. In a café, it's unlikely that we need to pay attention to anyone else, unlike in the office, where we may need to listen to something important.

If back working in open-plan offices, you need to train your hearing by disengaging the auditory system when you don't need to be on the lookout for important information.

Add some greenery

Research has shown that plants in your workspace can reduce your stress and can help you to think more clearly. We have an innate desire as humans to be connected to nature: this is called biophilia. Brain scans show that even just looking at pictures of green meadows for 40 seconds is enough to shift the brain into a more relaxed state. So, add a pot plant to your workspace!

Marie Kondo your workspace

While it's been reported that a messy desk helped Albert Einstein win a Nobel Prize, a clutter-free workspace is recommended for most of the tasks you might typically undertake in a day. A clutter-free workspace reduces the cognitive load, which in turn makes you more productive. A messy desk is a drain on your cognitive resources: your brain is constantly thinking about the mess, so you fatigue more quickly, which elevates your stress. Some studies also show it can lead to anxiety and depression.

Physical clutter can place unnecessary demands on your brain and cause feelings of overwhelm. When your desk is piled with paperwork, your diary (if you still have one) and a myriad of Post-it notes and digital devices, it's really challenging to stay focused. I can hear my mum's voice saying, 'A tidy desk, is a tidy mind'. Research confirms there's some truth to my mum's statement: A Princeton University study found that people performed poorly on cognitive tasks when objects in their field of vision were in disarray, as opposed to organised.

Micro-habit 3: Declutter your digital space

Visual clutter, such as a messy computer desktop or an overflowing or disorganised inbox, can unnecessarily add to your cognitive load. Your brain likes to conserve energy, so it craves order. Constant visual reminders of disorganisation therefore deplete your cognitive resources and impair your ability to focus. The cognitive overload caused by clutter can, in turn, reduce your working memory. Researchers have used functional magnetic resonance imaging (fMRI) and found that removing clutter from home and work environments results in increased ability to focus and process information, and bolstered productivity.

Here's what to try.

Remove your tech temptations

Your eyes are your dominant sense. What's in your line of sight is of critical importance. Another way to optimise your physical environment is to ensure that your physical workspace is conducive to working and not full of temptations that may distract or overwhelm you.

Stanford University psychologist BJ Fogg describes this as 'designing for laziness'. Basically, you're less likely to do things you *don't* want to if you make them less convenient. Try and create friction for your bad habits. For example, if you find yourself constantly reaching for your phone and scrolling social media or checking news sites, leave it in another room, pop it in a drawer or put it in a box. If you keep checking emails when you should be doing focused work, pause your inbox, disable the alerts or shut it down completely.

Equally, if you want to optimise your desirable habits, use visual cues that will nudge you to embed the habits. If you want to drink more water during the day, keep your full water bottle nearby.

Declare email bankruptcy

Seeing a pile of emails (either unread or read) can create stress. In the *How I Work* podcast with Dr Amantha Imber, Google Productivity Advisor Laura Mae Martin described having an inbox with 16,783 emails and only needing 45 of them as being like walking into your wardrobe with 4000 shirts but only ever wearing four of them. It's overwhelming and stressful.

Get everything you no longer need out of your inbox. If you have more than a couple of hundred emails in your inbox, then it's worth archiving your inbox and starting afresh.

Don't be a tab hoarder

Open your internet browser and check how many open tabs you currently have. I have 12 at the moment. Closing your tabs sounds like a very small thing you can do, but it has a profound impact, both in terms of wellbeing and productivity. The tab icons have been intentionally designed to be aesthetically appealing and captivating, so having them visible may distract you when you need to be doing focused work.

Declutter your desktop

Just as your physical space can add to your mental load if it's messy or cluttered, so too can your digital space. A desktop that is littered with so many folders, screenshots and documents that you can't actually see the lovely desktop image you once selected is overwhelming for your visual system.

Audit your downloads

In our haste to move through our digital days, many of us end up with cumbersome download folders. Who has time to check through their downloads folder? Well, not only will a huge downloads folder slow down your machine, but it can also add to your digital load.

Summary

1. Sit-stand-switch.
2. Set it up right.
3. Declutter your digital space.

PILLAR II

ADOPT NEURO-PRODUCTIVITY PRINCIPLES

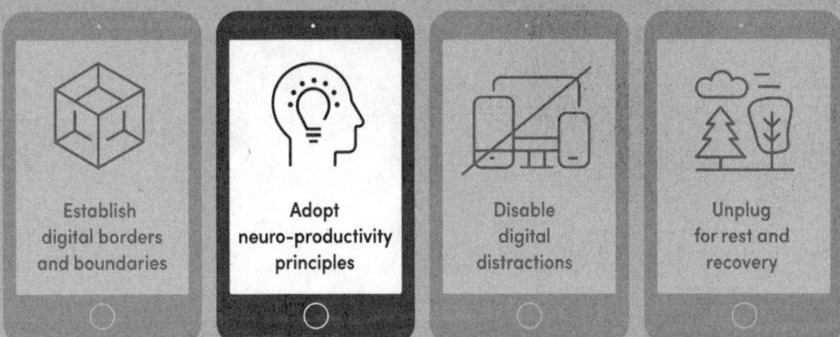

Have you ever tried to put together Ikea furniture without reading the step-by-step instructions? Even though you think it will be quite simple, it ends up being time-consuming and frustrating, and usually at the end you will have a wobbly piece of furniture.

The same is true for our brains. When we actually read the instructions and understand how the parts work best together, we can set up our workdays and use technology in ways that work for us. We can work more productively and look after our wellbeing when we work in congruence with our biological blueprint. That's exactly what this book decodes next: how to work productively according to how our brains and bodies function.

Pillar II explores how we can set up our workdays in ways that are aligned to our neurobiology. It covers the latest science about how we can structure our workdays so that they're compatible with what our brains and bodies need to function best. It explains why our brains are designed to work in digital dashes (sprints), not marathons, especially when working online. It also outlines why our teams should set up speedy meetings and what constitutes a 'restorative' break.

Pillar II examines three practices that enable us to work *with* our brain's biological needs:

1. Work in digital dashes.
2. Do deep work during peak-performance windows.
3. Mono-task, don't multi-task.

Practice 4

Work in digital dashes

Ben's workday used to start when he walked into the office at 8 a.m., coffee in hand, ready to attack the day. He'd plant himself on his office chair and go from one Teams meeting to the next, interspersing his meetings with quick inbox triages and chat messages. Before he knew it, it was 1:30 p.m. and he'd only left his chair once to go to the bathroom.

As his stomach started to grumble, Ben would remember that he'd forgotten to eat since the breakfast he'd slammed down before he left for work. He'd rush downstairs, grab a salad for lunch and bring it back to his desk, knowing there was a pile of emails he needed to plough through. Ben's afternoons were spent in more meetings (both hybrid and in person), and he'd finally tackle one of the critical to-dos on his list at 4 p.m. (when his energy was really fading and the sugar hit from his 3.30 p.m. biscuit had faded). Ben wouldn't leave his desk until 6 p.m., when he'd finally wrap up his office day. His third shift would start around 10 p.m., after having dinner with his partner, when he'd sit with his laptop on the lounge and watch Netflix while clearing his inbox… and lament all the tasks he simply didn't get done in his ten-plus-hour day.

Ben's day is typical of how many knowledge workers now spend their days (and nights). The COVID-19 pandemic has resulted in many of us working for increasing spans. According to Microsoft's 2022 Work Trend Index, the average Microsoft Teams user's workday has expanded by 13 per cent (or 46 minutes per day) since April 2020. Also concerning is that after-hours work has grown by 28 per cent and weekend work by 14 per cent.

This is *not* how we're biologically designed to work. The part of our brain that does most of our heavy lifting during the workday is our prefrontal cortex, which is one of the most energy demanding regions of the brain. This means we can realistically complete no more than six hours of cognitively challenging work each day. Punching out 14-hour days is working against our neurobiology and, if you do this, you'll see a deterioration in your performance, sometimes referred to as 'fatigability effect'.

We cannot outperform our biology. Humans need to take regular breaks; we cannot keep going and going without taking time to recharge and rest. In fact, we don't even expect machinery in factories to keep going without taking time for maintenance. Rest and working in short bursts, not long stretches, are integral to our performance.

So, let's explore how we can work *with* our human operating system (hOS) by meeting our brain's biological needs. These three micro-habits focus on why we need to work in short bursts when working online, why we experience Zoom fatigue (and some science-backed strategies to beat it), why it's critical to optimise our breaks and why we need to set our calendar default to speedy meetings.

Micro-habit 1: Set your work schedule in 90-minute intervals

One of the distinct biological markers we have as humans is our ultradian rhythm. This means our energy goes through peaks and troughs roughly every 90 minutes. This rhythm consists of measurable physiological patterns that our body maintains both day and night to manage the cycles of energy production and recovery. It is like a micro-version of our circadian rhythm (our 24-hour sleep-and-wake cycle), but much shorter and occurring multiple times each day. Like our circadian rhythm, if disrupted or ignored, our ultradian rhythm can really mess with our health and performance.

Here's how it typically plays out: you begin your day in a focused state and start to burn through glucose, a brain fuel. Within about 90 minutes, you reach what's described as your 'peak-performance window'. As you work, by-products build up in your brain in the form of metabolic waste and cellular debris. Your brain is also processing new bits of information. You may feel fatigued, groggy and frustrated, and your attention is likely to wander.

This is your body waving a red flag and telling you it needs some downtime to rest and recover. It's at this point that you've hit your ultradian trough, which is an energy low point. You'll probably crave one of the three Cs:

1. caffeine
2. carbs
3. crappy connections via social media. (The third C used to be cigarettes, but thankfully most of us have moved on.)

It's at this point that you need to take a break, as figure 4.1 shows. However, most of us ignore the signs from our bodies. We push through and don't rest during the ultradian trough. We disregard our bodies' signals and attempt to white-knuckle our way through our day. That's what I used to do, too, until I realised it was killing my productivity and having a detrimental impact on my mood, and leading me once again down the burnout path. Taking breaks is a responsibility, not a reward.

Figure 4.1: The ultradian rhythm

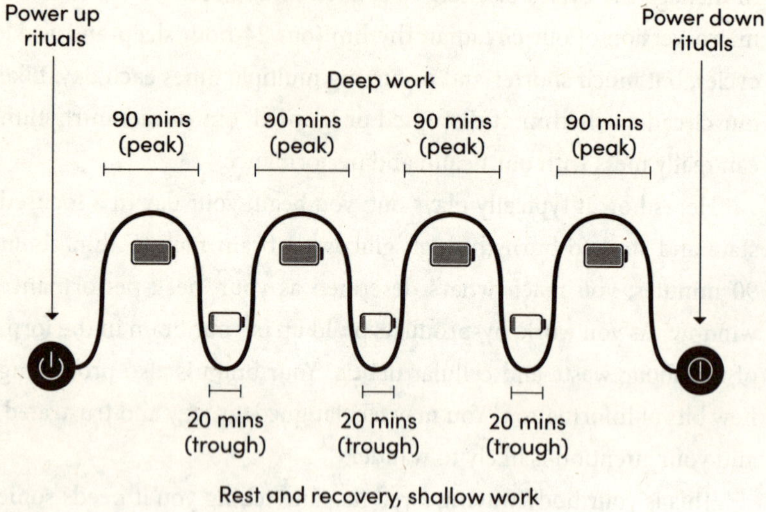

Skipping breaks results in the law of diminishing returns, which, as Greg McKeown discusses in his book *Effortless*, '… tells us that past a certain point, additional effort yields less results. What's worse, if we continue to double down on the "more effort approach" diminishing returns turn into negative returns. Additional effort can actually sabotage our performance.' Many of us are working in this way, and it's compromising our wellbeing and productivity.

If we skip subsequent breaks, we'll continue to feel blah – really blah! The more breaks you skip, the worse you'll feel, because you're working against your biology. By the end of the day, you'll fall in a heap. An always-on mind leaves you in a perpetual sympathetic-nervous-system state. Having a sympathetic nervous system stuck in a chronic stress response can disrupt your sleep, which further impedes your performance and compromises your mood and immunity. It becomes a vicious, self-perpetuating cycle that's hard to break. It's why many of us feel trapped and OUSTED.

Here are some simple yet effective ideas to help you work with your ultradian rhythm.

Determine your cadence

Your ultradian rhythm may not be exactly 90 minutes. The trick is to determine *your* ultradian rhythm. Start to notice when fatigue, lack of focus or fidgeting set in. It's likely a sign that you've hit your ultradian trough and it's time to take a break.

Time-block your calendar accordingly

Once you've determined your ultradian pattern, structure your day to match your rhythm. This gives you a basic plan for the day. You don't need to adhere rigidly to it, but having a time-blocked calendar removes some of the cognitive load that you typically assign to deciding what you need to do next and how long you should spend on that task.

Schedule breaks in your calendar

Set reminders in your calendar to take frequent breaks throughout the day. Remember, this can vary over time – it's not a precise science whereby you need to adhere strictly to your 82-minute ultradian rhythm or else everything implodes. You could even specify what you'll do during your break: walk the dog, walk to the postbox and mail a letter, lie in the sun, or do some squats and lunges.

Micro-habit 2: Optimise your breaks to optimise performance

The second phase of your ultradian rhythm, your trough, is integral to the success of your next ultradian peak. You cannot have one without the other. Your ultradian trough typically lasts for around 20 minutes. This is when your brain refuels with adenosine triphosphate, which stores and moves the energy in your cells. If you rest during your trough, or at least tackle some less demanding work, your brain has time to eliminate any toxins that were accumulating and process new information. This allows your brain to recharge and be ready to fire on all cylinders for the next 90 minutes or so. Whoop whoop!

However, if you fail to adhere to your biological needs during your trough, your productivity will plummet. Even your physical coordination will be hampered – you'll type more slowly, or you'll knock your coffee over your keyboard. You're more prone to accidents if you haven't taken sufficient breaks because your peripheral vision narrows, so you overlook things you'd typically notice. This is when you'll find yourself taking 45 minutes to complete an Excel formula that would usually take you ten minutes, or taking four attempts to rewrite the same paragraph because the words just aren't coming. You slog along, flogging your brain and body for the next 90 or so minutes. Your output suffers, and it's a recipe for exhaustion and burnout.

At this point you might be thinking, *Kristy I simply cannot get through my work if I'm stopping to take a 20-minute break every 90 minutes*. The good news is that you don't have to rest and do *nothing* for those 20 minutes. While it's true that your energy will wane during your ultradian trough, it doesn't mean you have to grind to a halt and sit in meditation. Some of that time should be devoted to restorative practices, and some could be dedicated to less taxing work such as replying to emails, returning phone calls while you go for a walk, and basic administration – what Cal Newport calls 'shallow work'.

The trick is to take 'good' breaks by including at least some of the following components in each break.

Restoration

I hate to say it, but finishing a meeting and pulling out your phone to check a news site, your inbox or social media is *not* restorative. Your brain needs a break. You need to do something that doesn't make demands of your prefrontal cortex. Could you do some deep breathing, go for a quick walk or make a cuppa?

Exposure to light

Ideally, you want to get some natural sunlight during your break, but even artificial light will activate your hypothalamus and have a positive impact on your attention, arousal and performance. Could you sit outside, find a sunny spot on your balcony or go for a walk outside and grab a coffee?

Movement

Basically, physical movement activates a range of neurotransmitters that not only make you feel good but also help you to focus. Could you have some go-to exercises that you do at home, such as walking lunges, resistance-band bicep curls, or even toe raises while the kettle boils? If you're stuck for ideas, google 'Lizzie Williamson's Two Minute Moves' for some great micro-movement ideas.

Nature

Time in nature has been shown to have a calming and restorative effect on the brain. Even just nature sounds can be restorative: one study found that participants who listened to chirping crickets and waves crashing performed better on cognitively demanding tasks than those who listened to traffic and busy café sounds. Could you close your eyes and sit outside, walk in your local park during your break without your earbuds in, or even pop your earbuds in and listen to a nature soundtrack?

Autonomy

Ideally, you want to have some control over how you spend your rest time. One study examined end-of-workday fatigue levels and found that fatigue was moderated by the degree of autonomous choice associated with lunchtime breaks.

Connection

Our most basic psychological need as humans is relational connection; we're biologically wired to be part of a tribe. We need time to connect with other humans. Hybrid and remote work have meant that we're not getting as much human interaction as we once did. Could you go for a walk with a colleague if you're back in the office, or organise to have a coffee with a friend, or simply pick up the phone and have a good old-fashioned conversation?

Micro-habit 3: Manage meetings better

I've spent countless hours over the last few years on Zoom, Teams and Webex calls. I've seen my share of Zoom-bombers (including my dad, who made a cameo while I was delivering a virtual keynote to several hundred people when he walked in to care for my napping toddler). I've been psychologically scarred by some of the things I've seen happening in the background of video calls, such as the naked partner who delivered his wife a coffee while she was presenting – instead of hitting the camera button, she hit the unmute button so all delegates could see and hear the chaos and panic unfolding.

A study found that Microsoft users have experienced a 252 per cent increase in time spent in meetings per week since February 2020, and the number of weekly meetings has increased by 153 per cent during this same period. We've become so accustomed to video calls that 'Zooming' has now become part of our vernacular. However, one thing that hasn't got any easier is dealing with Zoom fatigue.

Microsoft conducted several studies confirming that we find remote meetings more mentally exhausting, and there's science to explain why. One study involving heart-rate data and data from EEG machines showed that mental fatigue sets in around 30 to 40 minutes into a virtual meeting, and stress levels set in after about two hours into a day of video calls.

Other studies have looked at the cumulative impact of back-to-back virtual meetings. Microsoft examined what happened in the brain when people went from one meeting to another: for the participants who didn't have break periods, they observed beta activity (or stress levels) spiking. They attributed this to knowing as you were ending one meeting that another was looming, and that you'd have to switch gears to tackle another topic. For these participants, beta activity increased again when the next meeting started. In comparison, people who took ten-minute meditation breaks between virtual meetings saw a decline in beta brain activity and an increase at the start of the next meeting that was much smoother and gentler (see figure 4.2).

Figure 4.2: The impact on the brain of back-to-back meetings

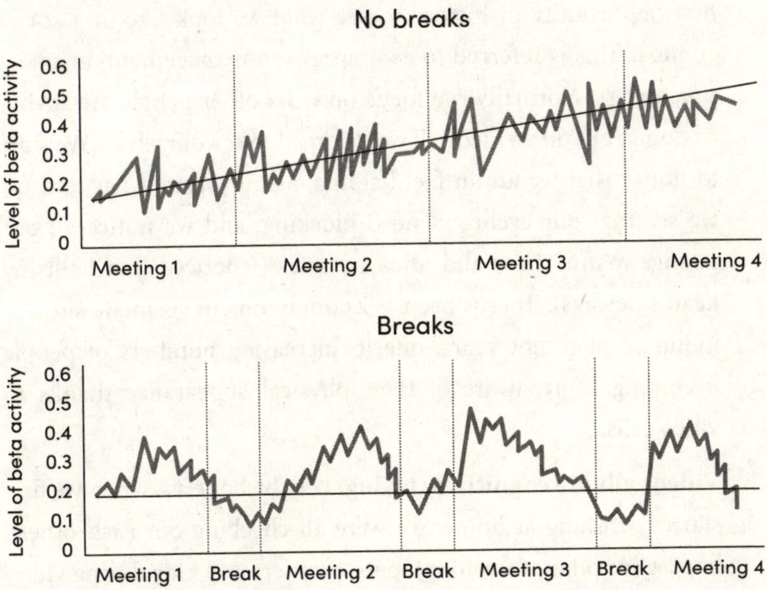

Chris Warhurst, Group CEO at Magic Memories, said:

> 'Within the maelstrom of the pandemic, most businesses responded with agility to survive and restart. The predominant feature was an accelerated adoption of existing video-conferencing and allied technology to facilitate team communication. The prevalence of video meetings allowed us to maintain an agile workspace and addressed some desire for employee flexibility, but the negatives in my view were an overscheduling of video meetings when compared to face-to-face requests and the diminishing of organic connection and collaboration folks achieve when in a shared physical environment.'

Several researchers, including the Virtual Human Interaction Lab at Stanford University, have studied why so many people found video calls taxing and tiring. Six common issues have been identified:

1. **Video self-presentation effect:** Video calls provide us with the first opportunity in history to see what we look like in a social context. This is referred to as 'impression management' in social psychology. Normally, we focus on what other people are saying or doing, but on a video call we're forced to see ourselves. We start to notice that we are in fact balding, as our partner has told us; we see that our eyebrows need plucking; and we notice all our strange mannerisms and idiosyncrasies (I noticed that I tilt my head sideways). There's been a 'Zoom boom' in cosmetic surgery inquiries in recent years, due to increasing numbers of people becoming more aware of their physical appearance thanks to video calls.
2. **Video calls are cognitively taxing:** Let's be honest – when we first started working at home, we were all checking out each other's houses (or piles of washing), pets, partners and kids during video

calls. Video calls mean that everyone is calling from different contexts: some of us are at home, some are in a shared working space and some are back in the office. These different contexts mean that our brains must work harder to process what we see. We also get a truncated, postage-stamp-sized view of other people, so we miss critical non-verbal cues such as gestures, body language and even micro facial expressions that we'd find easy to read if we were in the same room. To compensate, we often exaggerate our body movements, such as our nods and smiles, because we don't want our non-verbal cues to be misinterpreted. This is exhausting.

3. **Reduced mobility:** When we meet in person or chat via a phone call, we naturally move around and reposition ourselves. However, with video calls, most cameras have a limited field of view, meaning we must stay in the same spot and sit quite still. As we explored in Practice 2, limited mobility can not only reduce our creativity, but it can also increase our stress.

4. **Multi-tasking perils:** I'm sure we've all sat in meetings and thought, 'This meeting really could have been an email'. So often, we're tempted to multi-task during meetings by checking our inboxes, or Teams or Slack chats. Researchers from Amazon, Microsoft and University College London examined how frequently people multi-tasked in meetings and ascertained that people multi-task more frequently in larger and longer meetings (especially meetings that exceed 80 minutes). They also found that multi-tasking tends to occur more often in recurring meetings as opposed to ad hoc meetings, and we're more likely to multi-task in meetings in the morning than in the afternoon. Forty per cent of respondents said that they felt obliged to work during meetings to cope with the proliferation of virtual meetings that now peppered their calendars. Basically, we multi-task in meetings to cope with the incessant digital demands. Also, while we may deliberately

multi-task during video meetings, we are often doing it obliviously. Let's say you're working from home and your partner is there too. If they're on a video call while you are, it can split your attention; even though you know you should be focused on your meeting, your brain is also tuning into what they're saying.

5. **Social intensity:** When you meet a friend at a café to chat, you don't spend the entire conversation staring into each other's eyes the way you do during video calls. You look around; you notice the other guests at the café; you look up to see if the barista has made your order. Also, there are natural pauses in your conversation. You communicate with words and via your body language. Now, imagine you're on a Teams meeting with a colleague; if you look away from the screen, it feels rude. However, this close-up eye contact is exhausting. You're viewing someone's head at a very unnatural size and at a much closer distance than you normally would in person. This is stressful.

6. **Social awkwardness:** As a virtual speaker, I've delivered many a funny line and waited for the audience to laugh. Likewise, if we share a sad story, we expect people to respond appropriately. If we start to talk at the same time as someone else, we usually stop (or, at least, we're supposed to). However, video lags that are common on video calls can create awkwardness, because these social etiquettes get disrupted. A 2014 study found that a 1.2-second delay between when someone says something and when you respond can make people perceive you as less friendly. This, in turn, can fudge social etiquettes. Hand gestures, micro-expressions and lower body language are all much harder to read during video calls, especially if the cue only lasts for a fraction of a second.

So, what to do? Here are some easy ways to manage your virtual or hybrid meetings to beat Zoom fatigue.

Shorten your meetings

As a team, establish a meeting protocol that 60-minute meetings are now 50 minutes and 30-minute meetings are a standard 25 minutes. This allows people to have a buffer break between meetings to reduce stress and fatigue.

Set the meeting default in your calendar

Use your calendar software to make the default timing either 25 or 50 minutes. This removes any additional steps required to embed this habit and means that teams are more likely to adopt the practice if it's the calendar's default setting.

Make speedy meetings one of your team's digital guardrails

I've worked with many teams to help them establish their digital guardrails: the accepted norms, practices and behaviours that dictate how hybrid teams use digital technologies. Microsoft's 2022 Work Trend Index found that only 27 per cent of organisations have established hybrid meeting etiquette. These team agreements are critical to making hybrid work work. One hybrid meeting protocol might be that cameras are expected to be on during meetings unless otherwise specified.

Switch to phone calls

Over the last few years, I've sometimes suggested to clients or colleagues that we switch our video call to an old-fashioned phone call. The response has been staggering: people are simply relieved at the prospect of chatting over the phone as opposed to on video. Research has shown that social interactions that include voice, as compared to written text, create stronger social bonds without any increase in awkwardness. Another study from Yale University also found that voice-only interactions allow people to be more adept at reading social cues. It appears that our vocal cues can be a strong indicator of our mental state.

Breaks to remember

If I gave you a long list of animals to remember and told you that you needed to recall them *without* writing them down, how many could you recall? Let's give it a go: donkey, cat, whale, sheep, tiger, giraffe, kitten, hippo, lion, bear, eagle, pig, elephant. Chances are, you're likely to remember the first couple and perhaps the last couple, but the middle is a little messy. Our brains are efficient and know they won't recall the 34 to 74 gigabytes worth of data that come their way each day, so we tend to remember the beginning and end of chunks of information. This is referred to as the 'primacy/recency effect'. When you take more breaks, you artificially contrive more beginnings and endings (as figure 4.2 illustrates), so your recall of information will be stronger.

Summary

1. Set your work schedule in 90-minute intervals.
2. Optimise your breaks, boost your performance.
3. Manage meetings better.

Practice 5

Do deep work during peak-performance windows

After attending a conference and hearing a productivity speaker, Matt joined the 5 a.m. club, waking up early to tackle his work. This speaker, like many productivity gurus, espoused doing your most challenging tasks first up in the day, and listed off names of highly productive people who claim to start their days early and dive straight into their deep work. This is 'eating the frog', a term popularised by Brian Tracy, and it's a popular piece of productivity advice.

However, it's flawed advice. Like Matt, not everyone fires on all cylinders early in the morning. In fact, it's estimated that only a small proportion of people (around 15 per cent) are early risers. Matt certainly wasn't. He'd wake up early to do his most taxing work first, yet he felt unfocused and exhausted.

I delivered a series of masterclasses to Matt and his team during the pandemic. One of the micro-habits I shared was to schedule your day to match your chronotype. Your chronotype determines when you're most alert and focused, and dictates when you'd naturally like to fall asleep. I suggested to Matt and his team that if they worked with their biology, they would optimise their performance. Matt was reluctant to try it at first, because it was almost antithetical to the productivity advice he'd previously been given and counter to mainstream productivity advice.

Matt took a chronotype assessment and determined that he was a 'bear', meaning that his peak-performance window was typically between 10 a.m. and 3 p.m. No wonder he struggled to do his deep work at 5 a.m., as this was well outside his peak-performance window. Matt started to structure his day to work *with* his chronotype. As a result, Matt's output increased exponentially. He started to fiercely protect his time between 10 a.m. and 1 p.m. most days, reserving this for his most mentally demanding work. He tried to avoid meetings during his peak-performance window when possible, and he put in place some simple strategies (covered in this practice) to build a fortress around his focus during this window.

Let's discover when your peak-performance window is (based on your chronotype) and how you can leverage this to optimise your performance.

Micro-habit 1: Work in concert with your chronotype

As mentioned, your chronotype is your unique biological rhythm that determines at what time of the day or night you're most alert and focused. It governs when you naturally want to fall asleep and when you're most energetic. Related to your circadian rhythm, your chronotype controls your sleep-wake cycle and production of the sleep hormone melatonin. Unlike your circadian rhythm, which is governed by your exposure to light, your chronotype isn't shaped by any external forces: it's genetically determined by your PER3 gene and, as such, it can't be easily shifted, although it does often change over the course of a lifetime. Your chronotype can be shaped by your habits, but only by one or two hours.

Traditionally, people were classified as larks (early risers), hummingbirds (neither early nor late risers) and owls (late risers). Psychologists and sleep specialists used a Morningness-Eveningness Questionnaire (MEQ) to determine an individual's chronotype. However, more recent research suggests that there are likely to be more chronotypes. Dr Michael Breus suggests in his book *The Power of When* that there are four distinct chronotypes:

1. **Lions** are morning-oriented people with a medium sleep drive.
2. **Bears** have a solar-based schedule and a high sleep drive.
3. **Wolves** are night-oriented people with a medium sleep drive.
4. **Dolphins** have a low sleep drive and tend to be insomniacs.

Historically, the traditional workday that was based on a nine-to-five work schedule really only suited bears, who account for around 50 per cent of the population. We now have an opportunity to align our chronotype with our work demands and find rhythms that work for lions (15 to 20 per cent of the population) and wolves (15 to 20 per cent of the population).

If you consider your chronotype and your traditional work hours pre-pandemic, there's a strong probability that there was a misalignment. In fact, one sleep expert has proposed that prior to the pandemic, 80 per cent of people had work schedules that conflicted with their chronotype.

We're not designed to follow a rigid, one-size-fits-all routine. I believe the silver lining of the pandemic for knowledge workers is that we now have far greater flexibility in *when* we work. While much focus has been given to flexible work arrangements, I believe that the real opportunity lies in creating productive work arrangements. In a 2022 report by Future Forum, 94 per cent of employees were demanding schedule flexibility. If organisations want to attract and retain talent, flexible work arrangements are no longer just a bullet point in policies, but rather a critical component of employee value propositions. Offering genuine flextime – going beyond it just being a buzzword in your employee handbook – will create a healthier, more productive workforce.

While some occupations and roles are time- and location-dependent, many are not. Even in roles that are time-dependent, employees do have some control over the types of tasks they perform at certain times. If we can align our work schedules according to when we're most productive, we can optimise our performance and wellbeing.

For example, Southwest Airlines allows pilots to choose between morning and evening flight schedules. The U.S. Navy changed their existing 18-hour schedule to a 24-hour one that suited the sailors' biological rhythms. These decisions have implications for safety (fatigued workers are much more likely to make errors), wellbeing and performance.

A real-world experiment was conducted at ThyssenKrupp, a German steel manufacturer, whereby the early risers were assigned to the day shift and the night owls were given the late shift. By aligning their work schedules to their chronotypes, people got 16 per cent more sleep, which equated to almost a full night's sleep over the course of a week. This had profound impacts on their rest and performance. Another study involving healthcare workers found that employees derived more joy from their work if their rostered shifts matched their chronotype's peak window.

A McKinsey & Company study found that executives who carved out their peak-performance hours believed they were five times more productive at their peak than during their average working time. However, most reported that they were only in their peak zone for less than 10 per cent of their working time. The report suggested that if employees increased the duration of their peak time by a modest 20 per cent, their overall workplace productivity would almost double.

Time flexibility not only bolsters people's productivity but also allows people with chronic illness to attend doctor's appointments or have a rest in the middle of the day without them needing to take a sick day. It is also beneficial for working parents who can attend school sporting carnivals or assemblies in lieu of taking time off.

Here are some top tips for working with your chronotype.

Determine if you're a bear, wolf, lion or dolphin

Most of us intuitively know our chronotype. I suggest that you can identify yours by what time you naturally want to fall asleep and wake up when you're about four days into your holidays, with no alarms and schedules dictating your time. If you still need a bit of help, then I've developed an online tool to identify your chronotype in the Book Resources section of my website.

Devote your focus hours to your most intellectually demanding tasks

Fence off your most productive hours in your calendar. Where possible, avoid meetings and digital distractions during your chronotype's peak-performance window, which should be devoted to your deep work. When you align your work tasks with when your energy is at its peak, you're far more productive.

Follow a sleep schedule that matches your chronotype's biological needs

There's no use following a work schedule that matches your chronotype's needs if you're not also following the corresponding sleep schedule. Each chronotype has a unique sleep schedule that you should adhere to (see figure 5.1).

Figure 5.1: Chronotype sleep schedules

	Lion	Bear	Wolf	Dolphin
Ideal wake time	6 a.m.	7 a.m.	9 a.m.	6.30 a.m.
Ideal sleep time	10 p.m.	11 p.m.	1 a.m.	11.30 p.m.
Peak performance window	6 a.m.– 11 a.m.	10 a.m.– 3 p.m.	5 p.m.– 10 p.m.	3 p.m.– 9 p.m.

Based on *The Power of When* by Michael Breus, PhD

Set core collaboration hours

One of the challenges facing teams with employees that have different schedules is the lack of common collaboration time. Project bottlenecks can result if people don't have time to collaborate in real time. Teams can overcome this by specifying core collaboration hours. For example, Dropbox has core collaboration hours, whereby a block of time is specified for team members to be online and available. The rest of the day is determined by the employee. On its Virtual First policy documents, Dropbox states, 'Asynchronous work means the job can get done any time, not just during "work hours"'.

Micro-habit 2: Triage your to-do list

Many of us have a master to-do list, which is a brain sneeze of all the tasks we need to accomplish written on a long list. (Nikki Elledge Brown introduced me to the term brain sneeze rather than brain 'dump', which, for a mum of three boys, has all sorts of negative connotations.) It might include big tasks, such as data analysis or creating a proposal, alongside much less taxing and time-consuming tasks, such as replying to a client email, making a phone call or organising a Zoom meeting. We don't discriminate between the types of tasks and the complexities they pose. This means looking at our to-do list is often an onerous and overwhelming experience; ironically, our to-do lists often further add to our sense of overwhelm and infobesity.

A more effective method is to create a triaged to-do list using a special process I've developed (illustrated in figure 5.2) that combines two well-known productivity approaches: Cal Newport's 'deep' and 'shallow' work, and the Eisenhower Matrix that classifies tasks according to their urgency and importance.

Figure 5.2: Triaging your to-do list

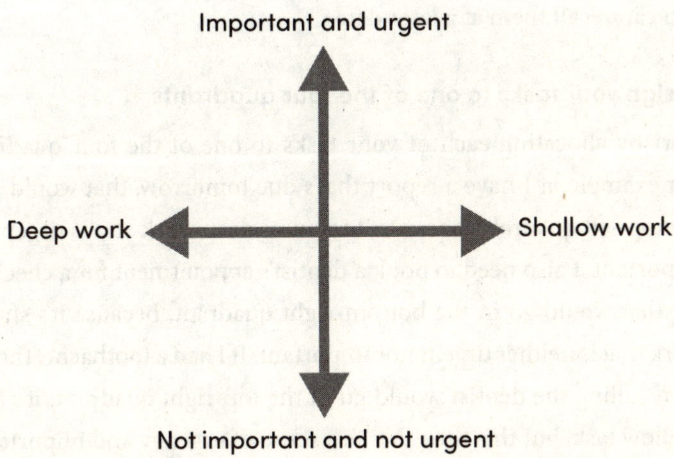

To triage your to-do list using this method, take the following steps.

Identify tasks that are both urgent and important

Start by asking yourself if the tasks you're going to perform that day or week (whatever timeframe you're planning around) are both urgent *and* important. The original Eisenhower framework classified tasks into four domains: urgent, not urgent, important and not important. This was a great model for the era in which it was developed, but we need to refine it for current times given the overwhelming amount of choice and information we now have at our fingertips (which can make *everything* feel important and urgent). I suggest that for a task to make it to your to-do list, it must be both urgent *and* important.

This is not to suggest that non-urgent or unimportant tasks aren't to be performed. However, those tasks should be delegated when possible or added to a different list called the delayed list. We definitely need to keep track of delayed or delegated tasks, because our brains have finite cognitive capabilities, so chances are they won't be able to recall them. However, they're not tasks we need to attend to urgently, and so putting them on our to-do lists will only serve to overwhelm us. Instead, save them in a journal, Trello board or Word document so you can recall them at a later date.

Assign your tasks to one of the four quadrants

Start by allocating each of your tasks to one of the four quadrants. For example, if I have a report that's due tomorrow, that would go in the top-left quadrant, because it requires deep work and is urgent and important. I also need to book a dentist's appointment for a check-up. So, that would go in the bottom-right quadrant, because it's shallow work that is neither urgent nor important. If I had a toothache, though, then calling the dentist would go in the top-right quadrant: it's still a shallow task, but this time there's a sense of urgency and importance.

Use your pre-meeting time wisely

Let's say you have 20 minutes spare before your next Zoom meeting. Researchers have found that free time seems shorter to people when it comes before a task or appointment, and that we're 22 per cent less productive before a meeting. Many of us whittle the time away unproductively – tell me I'm not the only one who uses this time to make another cup of tea, or hang out some washing when working remotely, or even check social media?

Instead, you could use that time to tick off some of the shallow tasks on your to-do list: return some emails, make a quick call, or scan and sign a document.

Keep your to-do list handy

I'm sure you've experienced what it's like to be fully engrossed in your work. You're in the flow state. Then, suddenly, you remember that a team member is waiting on a report that you agreed to send them. Many of us would then open our email, locate the file and send the link to our colleague, then go back to the work we were doing. By then, though, our flow state has vanished, and it's nearly impossible to get reoriented into the deep work mode again.

When random thoughts pop into your head while you're doing deep work, jot them down on your to-do list. (Alternatively, I sometimes find random thoughts appear at the most inopportune times and they're *not* actually tasks that need to go on my to-do list, so these go in my 'ideas to park' document or book.) This will greatly reduce your cognitive load and also prevent the 3 a.m. wakeups when you remember a task that you've forgotten to jot down.

Micro-habit 3: Build a fortress around your focus

While digital intruders are one of the chief culprits of distraction, there are other sources, too. Let's look at one source of distraction in particular: people. (We all have a chatty Cathy or talkative Tom in the office.)

In the early days of COVID-19 lockdowns in Sydney, before I'd built my studio, I had to deliver virtual keynotes from home with three young boys (ranging from 18 months to 10 years old). My husband was (conveniently) deemed an 'essential worker' and so wasn't at home to help. Delivering keynotes with three young kids in tow was no mean feat. These keynotes took place at the dining table, where two of the three boys also attempted (I use that word very loosely) to complete their remote learning.

On one occasion, I was presenting to over 750 people via Zoom. I'd set the two older boys up with some online learning tasks to keep them busy and given the toddler, who'd just learned to walk, a basket of toys to keep him occupied on the floor. It was a 20-minute presentation, and I thought, *surely I could focus for just 20 minutes.* Boy was I wrong! Just when I thought I'd nailed it, chaos erupted. The toddler managed to climb onto the dining table. His older brothers tried to 'silently' wrestle him off the table – because they knew that I had to keep presenting and couldn't be distracted – but he pushed them away, removed his nappy and did a poo on the dining table… all while the show went on! Talk about a shitshow!

It was nearly impossible for me to focus on the keynote. My attention was fractured. *Do I deal with the toddler mess? Do I acknowledge what's happening on the other side of my laptop? Do I keep presenting?* I think I was too traumatised to share what had just happened, so I just kept presenting. I finished the keynote and the client assured me during the post-event call that they had no idea what had taken place on the other side of my camera, but they did have a good laugh.

This is a prime example of why being interrupted is stressful. We intuitively know that we need to eliminate as many distractions as possible when we need to focus on a task. Tell me I'm not the only one who turns off the radio or podcast when driving to a new destination (or yells at the kids in the back seat to be quiet).

This concept is explored in much more detail in Pillar III, but here are my best tips to build a fortress around your focus during your peak-performance window to stop people from distracting you.

Use a sign to indicate that you're doing deep work

Put a Do Not Disturb sign on your door or desk, whether you're at home or in the office. Besides keeping intruders at a distance, Do Not Disturb signs can also be a source of humour. Alternatively, you could invest in a coloured red-green light to indicate when you're doing focused work. There is a plethora of Do Not Disturb light systems (also referred to as 'busy lights') for both corporate and home offices. These can be mounted to your computer, door or workspace and leave little room for any ambiguity about when you can be disturbed.

Wear specific clothes or a hat to signal that you're working when working from home

I've worn a baby pink mohair cardigan every time I've worked on this book. Yes, even on warmer days I'd still put it on, even if just for a short period of time. It was a clear cognitive signal that I was in book-writing mode, even if I was working in a hotel room, an airport lounge or at my dining table. It also sent a clear signal to my family to stay away!

For another example, during the pandemic, while I was working at home with three kids, I wore a fluorescent safety vest when I was working. This was a direct way of communicating with my sons that I couldn't be distracted. When I was wearing this vest, the kids knew that the 3B rule applied: they could only interrupt Mum if someone wasn't *breathing*, someone was *bleeding* or if someone had a *broken bone*.

One day, when I was doing a podcast interview, my son Billy stood on the side of the camera and kept saying, 'Mum! Mum!' I glanced away from the video to quickly scan Billy: no shortness of breath and no sign of bleeding or a broken bone, so I kept answering the podcast questions. But Billy kept trying to get my attention. I glanced sideways when he said, 'Mum, it's one of the Bs.' Panic set in. 'Mum, I'm going for a bike ride.' To him, that was the fourth B!

Work behind a closed door

Whether you're in the office or working at home, try to find a workspace with a door when you need to complete focused work. The door is a physical barrier that clearly signals that you can't be disturbed. I've even seen someone in a Sydney office use a sign that said, 'I'm in here. You're out there. Let's keep it that way until I decide to open the door.' Direct and effective.

Have open office hours

Having specified open hours, when your colleagues are invited to drop by your office (or come to your open Zoom or Teams meeting if you're doing this remotely), not only stops people from interrupting you at your desk but also drastically reduces the number of digital chats. Instead of firing off an email or sending a Teams chat, encourage people to write down what they want to talk to you about and bring it to you during your open office hours. An executive I worked with implemented this strategy and saw a whopping 42 per cent decrease in internal emails and 55 per cent decline in Teams chats over a one-month period. Have a sign on your office or use your email signature to remind people when your open office hours are scheduled.

Train people to stop interrupting you

When people come up to your desk and ask, 'Do you have a minute?' (and then 40 minutes later you're *still* chatting), be prepared to say 'No', or 'Not now'. (Open office hours can help with this as well.)

Wear noise-cancelling headphones while you work

Noise-cancelling headphones send an overt signal to your colleagues not to interrupt you. (More on this later.)

Have a communications policy

Clearly communicate with your colleagues about how they can reach out to you. Articulate your preferred communication mode (do you prefer email, Slack chats or a text message?) and your standard response rate. Atlassian suggests creating a one-page document that outlines your preferred communication modes and linking to it in your email signature, or sharing it with new team members.

Summary

1. Work in concert with your chronotype.
2. Triage your to-do list.
3. Build a fortress around your focus.

Practice 6

Mono-task, don't multi-task

Doctors and nurses prescribing and administering the wrong medications and dosages cause hundreds of thousands of preventable injuries in hospitals and billions of dollars in extra medical costs each year. Staff at the USCF Medical Center investigated why there were such high rates of medication errors and discovered that doctors and nurses were often multi-tasking while doing medication rounds: they would also be talking to a patient, or being interrupted by a colleague or a beeping machine. Their attention was split. Despite what we often tell ourselves, our brains are physiologically incapable of multi-tasking.

The USCF team came up with a low-cost intervention: they had their staff wear fluorescent 'do not interrupt' vests while performing medication rounds, like the vests worn by high-rise construction workers. What resulted was a staggering 88 per cent reduction in medication errors. By putting in place a physical, tangible reminder to avoid multi-tasking, the staff were able to bolster their focus and subsequent performance.

Now, apply that to your context and imagine, what is multi-tasking costing you? (Hopefully not lives, but it depends where you work, right?)

Numerous studies confirm that we cannot do two activities at the same time with sufficient focus; we can't multi-task. Instead, the human brain 'task-switches' constantly between the two different demands vying for its attention – and it doesn't switch all that well. This is referred to as the 'task-switching cost'.

Multi-tasking, or task switching, produces cortisol (the stress hormone) and adrenaline, which can inhibit learning and memory. Multi-tasking results in fatigue, because it depletes glucose levels in the brain. Stressed and exhausted brains don't allow neural pathways to form, because the brain thinks it's under threat and prioritises survival. Today, the pings, alerts and notifications from our devices are constantly vying for our attention and are elevating our stress response.

Multi-tasking also adversely impacts our memory. When we multi-task, we don't recruit the hippocampus, the memory centre of the brain; instead, we use the striatum, which is the brain system that underpins the acquisition of new skills, especially motor skills.

Much like our computer hard drives, our brains have a finite storage capacity. This is our 'cognitive load', and multi-tasking basically causes it to reach its threshold very quickly.

It's not just the initial distraction that's costly: there are also some delayed costs associated with interruptions. Studies have suggested that it takes adults an average of 23 minutes and 15 seconds to reorient their attention after a distraction. This is called the 'resumption lag'. For example, you're writing a report and your phone rings, and you take a two-minute call. When you go back to writing your report, it takes a long time (roughly 23 minutes) to get your brain back into that deep, focused state. Not only did you lose the two minutes that you took on the call but the 23 minutes it took afterwards to reorient your attention and resume the deep, focused state you were in before the interruption. Imagine the cumulative cost of such distractions throughout our modern workdays.

There are considerable financial costs associated with constant digital distractions, particularly around employee productivity. Distractions are posing significant financial costs to organisations, as this Economist Intelligence Unit data suggests:

- Twenty-eight per cent of working hours in knowledge work are lost to distractions in the USA.
- An average of 581 hours per knowledge worker is lost annually to distractions.
- Disruptions translate to US companies losing $391 billion annually in lost productivity in the sectors analysed.

One of the opportunities that hybrid and remote work offers is the ability to work in an *asynchronous* fashion: you're no longer bound to the nine-to-five workday in an office, so you don't have to be working at the same time as your colleagues. You can send an email and a colleague will reply when *they* are free. You can post a thread in a Teams chat and the person you tagged will respond at a time that works for *them*. You can pose a question in a project management tool and receive a response *later*.

However, many people and organisations are trying to use these asynchronous tools in a *synchronous* way – for example, by sending a colleague an email and then sending them a Teams message two hours later when an email reply hasn't come through (see figure 6.1). Some of us are spending our entire days in Teams or Slack and not getting any deep work done (until we can finally tackle it at 10 p.m.).

Figure 6.1: An unhelpful follow-up message

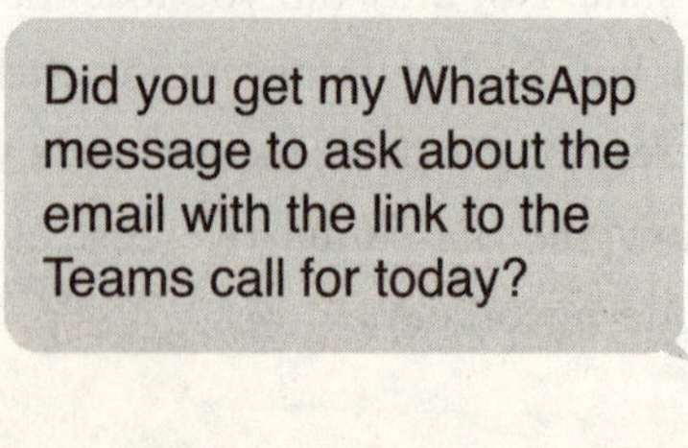

However, just as the staff at the USCF Medical Center discovered, when we work *with* our biological constraints, our performance improves. Rather than constantly switching tasks and splitting our attention, we can conserve our brain's resources by mono-tasking instead, using the three micro-habits in this practice to help.

Micro-habit 1: Plan your workday

As previously explored, we need to structure our workdays so that we build a fortress around our mental prime time: our peak-performance window of the day. We need to plan our days in advance by time-blocking our calendars and doing our deep, focused work during our peak-performance window. In his book *Indistractable*, Nir Eyal refers to this as 'timeboxing'; he suggests that if we don't control our time according to our values and schedule, then someone else will (or our inboxes will rule our days!).

When you intentionally plan your day, you won't be in and out of your inboxes or constantly checking your Slack messages: you'll have designated times of the day for shallow tasks such as asynchronous communication.

If you timebox your days hour by hour, you're much more likely to mono-task. If you revert to an open, unscheduled calendar, you're much more likely to revert to multi-tasking, because your brain craves the quick dopamine hit that comes from checking an email or scrolling social media.

Here are some tips to plan and structure your workday to optimise your chances of mono-tasking.

Establish your core collaboration hours

Establish core collaboration hours, like the teams at Dropbox. Dropbox has an expectation that team members will be online and available for certain specified hours each day, and that is when synchronous work takes place. Employees can set their own work hours and undertake tasks accordingly outside of those mandated collaboration hours. This gives employees dedicated times to collaborate (preventing project bottlenecks from occurring when people are working different hours) while also meeting the demands for employee flexibility.

Tess, who works at an insurance company, told me that her team determined core collaboration hours of between 1 and 2.30 p.m. each Monday, Wednesday and Thursday after I worked with them to establish their digital guardrails. This reduced their internal team emails by 78 per cent and their Slack chats by a whopping 81 per cent. It gave them much more time for deep work and adequate time to connect with their colleagues in real time to move projects forward.

Set and stick to your schedule

As you can see in figure 6.2, Lauren has set her deep work hours at the start of the day and her shallow work towards the end of the day to match her chronotype (she's a 'lion').

Figure 6.2: A 'lion' work plan

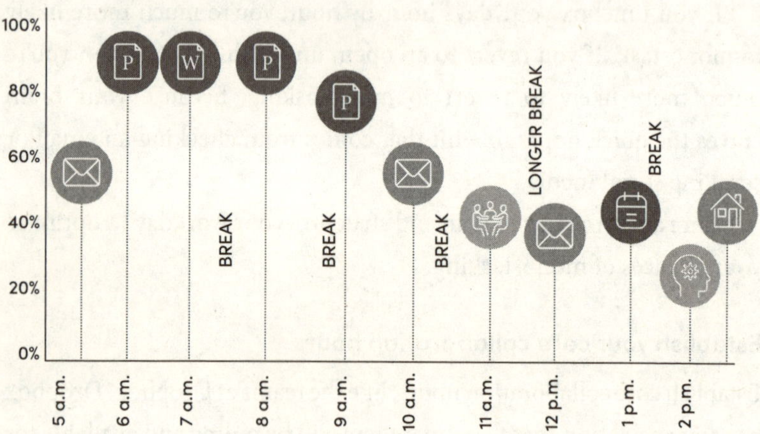

Having such a prescriptive approach to time management also gives Lauren the ability to protect her focus hours, so she's much less likely to accept meetings in the morning or engage in shallow work unless it's absolutely critical that they occur at this time.

Mute your collaboration notifications

Hearing the ping of a Teams notification or Slack message can distract you, even if you don't open it. You may start to ruminate on what the message regarded. So, mute them.

Timebox your day

Parkinson's Law is the adage that work expands to fill the time you allocate to it. If you take control of your calendar and timebox your most productive hours for your deep work, you'll plough through your work.

Micro-habit 2: Snack (don't nibble) on your inbox

Having worked with thousands of leaders, executives and employees over the years, I've found that email is still many people's Achilles heel. Email can dominate our work time, derail our productivity and diminish our mental wellbeing if we're not careful. A client of mine recently revealed that she realised her email habits had slipped into unhealthy territory when she found herself reading a colleague's email on the toilet (#toilettweeting).

Nibbling on emails throughout the day can dent our productivity. A study by RescueTime found that the average knowledge worker checks their emails and instant messages every six minutes. Six minutes! This study examined 185 million hours of knowledge workers' time and found that, on average, knowledge workers were able to carve out only two hours and 48 minutes of productive work time each day. It's near impossible to accomplish any type of cognitively taxing or 'deep' work if you're perpetually checking communication tools.

Unless your primary role requires immediate customer care or you're relying on time-critical information, there's no need to *constantly* check and respond to emails. Email is *not* a synchronous communication tool, and it was never designed to be our primary tool of communication. It's an asynchronous tool that should be supplemented with other communication tools: for example, if someone needs an urgent response from you, then calling you or sending a WhatsApp or Slack message may be a better choice. (This should be outlined in your Communication Escalation Plan, so there's only one agreed-upon mode of communication for time-sensitive, critical information.)

One of the most essential digital guardrails we can establish is how we use email. Use these tips to help.

Schedule when you'll check emails

Ideally, you should be checking emails at set times of the day, *outside* your peak-performance window. (Don't use your peak-performance window to respond to emails, because emails are 'shallow' work for most knowledge workers.) See the previous practice on how to identify your peak-performance window.

Let's use Lauren's time-blocked calendar as an example. She'd be best placed to do only a quick triage of her inbox just before 6 a.m. Because her peak-performance window is in the morning, she needs to reserve as much of this time as possible for her deep, focused work. This quick morning inbox triage would just be to ascertain if there is anything urgent that she needs to be across before she begins her day.

Lauren's colleague Sarah, who is a bear, starts her workday at 9.30 a.m. and, unlike Lauren, *would* be advised to start her workday by checking emails and responding to as many as she can during this time, because her peak-performance window is typically between 10 a.m. and 2 p.m.

Treat your email like laundry

Laura Mae Martin, a Google Productivity Expert, suggests that we treat our inboxes like laundry.

We wouldn't wash one sock, put it in the dryer and return it to the appropriate drawer, and then start the same process again for a t-shirt. Instead, we'd wait until we had a full load, sort the clothes by lights and darks, wash the clothes in loads, dry them and *then* sort them out. We need to batch-process our emails by going into our inboxes at set times of the day and sorting out the emails. We can reply to any emails that require two minutes of our time or less and file the rest to deal with at assigned times. Then, we need to assign specific times when we'll attack our most important folders.

Check email two to four times per day

When it comes to attacking those folders, research confirms that checking email two to four times per day is optimal, because it allows workers to be responsive and not reactive. Another study found that checking emails three times a day reduced employee stress. So, it appears that the happy medium for checking email is somewhere between two and four times per day, not every six minutes as many of us do.

Now, restricting your email-checking to four periods a day may not be achievable for you because of the demands of your job, but try to resist the urge to multi-task by nibbling on your inbox throughout the day, and instead assign specific windows when you intentionally check it. Allocate this time in your calendar each day so you're much more likely to adhere to it.

Set up a five-folder method

When doing your initial triage of your inbox (sorting your emails like laundry), sort the emails into five folders: 'Do', 'Digest', 'Delegate', 'Dump' and 'Documents'. Remember, only deal with emails that require two minutes of your time or less, and then file the rest to complete during your assigned email time in your calendar (which should be during one of your shallow work periods). There are further resources to help you tame your inbox in the Book Resources section of my website.

Manage people's tech-spectations

Use your email signature to clearly communicate how frequently you reply to emails. If there are extenuating circumstances that mean you'll be much less responsive, use your out-of-office message to communicate this.

Micro-habit 3: Wear noise-cancelling headphones

You know the drill: you start your Zoom meeting and, without fail, your next-door neighbour starts their leaf blower, your dog starts to bark, or your kids start to argue in the background. To combat the impact of background noise on video calls, Microsoft deployed background noise reduction capabilities in video calls using artificial intelligence (AI). However, the AI feature was so sophisticated that, while it solved the problem by removing background noise, it also created another problem, which has been referred to as the 'leaf blower problem'.

The leaf blower problem occurs during video meetings when there's a loud background noise for one participant, and the AI successfully eliminates that noise for other participants but *not* for the person with the loud background noise. While other participants can't hear the background sound, the person where the noise is emanating from can still hear it, and they're distracted by it. As a result, the other participants who can't hear the sound are bewildered as to why the person appears agitated, distracted or frustrated. The confusion can be magnified when this person apologises for the background noise that the other participants can't hear.

Research has confirmed that hearing intelligible speech can reduce our cognitive performance. It has also been shown to increase our stress. Why? Because this is a form of multi-tasking, and remember, our brains release cortisol when we're multi-tasking.

So, what happens in an open-plan office (or open-plan home)? Studies have confirmed what many office-bound workers know: open-plan offices can be stressful places to work and detrimental to our mood if they're not acoustically treated or well designed. When hearing background sounds, even if we're not paying attention to the sounds, our brains perceive this as a threat, resulting in us feeling stressed.

Prior to the pandemic, it was estimated that 70 per cent of office-based employees worked in open-plan offices. Complaints about noise and the logistics of such configurations were rife. Poor acoustic treatments and poor spatial planning can be to blame in such offices – not all open-plan offices are doomed. However, our rapid shift to hybrid work means that we now not only have noisy offices to contend with (which is amplified in offices where people are spending the bulk of their workdays in Zoom meetings), but we also potentially have distracting home offices, too (if we're lucky enough to have a home office).

A study by Bond University in experimentally controlled conditions using heart rate, skin conductivity and AI facial emotion recognition found a significant causal relationship between open-plan office noise and physiological stress. In fact, background noise heightened negative mood by 25 per cent – and these results came from just eight minutes of observation in open-plan office simulations. In a real office, where workers are exposed to noise continuously throughout the day, we can expect the effects on stress and mood to be even greater.

Dr Libby Sander, an Assistant Professor at Bond Business School, said:

> 'Open-plan offices are too often designed in a one-size-fits-all approach. This often means acoustic treatments that can assist with noise are limited or left out of the design altogether. Noise in open-plan offices has been shown in our research to have significant effects on an individual's ability to concentrate, on their mood, and on their physiological stress.'

Wearing noise-cancelling headphones will block out some of the superfluous background noise that distracts you and drains your cognitive resources. They can also send a powerful visual cue to your colleagues (or partners, or kids) that you don't want to be disturbed. They're as effective as putting a Post-it note on your forehead that says 'Do Not Disturb'.

One study found that wearing headphones alone wasn't sufficient to mask distractable background speech, so here are some other ideas to help.

Music to your ears

Carefully curated playlists, which you use exclusively when you work, *can* help you focus. You may have heard of the 'Mozart effect', which showed that listening to classical music improves your cognitive performance. However, the effects are only applicable to classical music, and you only see a small bump in improved focus for roughly 15 minutes.

Soft, slow and no lyrics

The music we listen to when we work should be soft, so our attention isn't dominated by overbearing sound. It should be relatively slow paced to imitate our resting heart rate of approximately 60 to 80 beats per minute. Dr Sahar Yousef shared in a video series with Headspace that listening to lyricless music or music with lyrics in a foreign language can help, because the language (or absence of it) doesn't interfere with your focus. Studies have shown that music with lyrics can hamper concentration and comprehension.

The trick with using music to optimise focus is that you must be careful to *only* listen to the playlist (at the gym, in the car, and so on), when you want to enter a highly focused state, because your brain can attenuate to it – if you constantly listen to the playlist, it will lose its potency and impact. You want your brain to make the mental association that it's time to work.

Brain.fm and Focus@Will have designed music dedicated to bolstering focus.

Listen to binaural beats

Binaural beats are a specific type of music that has been proven to boost focus and improve memory. Binaural beats are auditory illusions that occur when you hear different frequency sounds in different ears. Binaural beats at 40 hertz can put you in an alert, focused state, because the time difference between the signals arriving in the ear activates the prefrontal cortex. Binaural beats increase striatal dopamine in the brain, resulting in you blinking more, which in turn puts you in an alert state. Avoid listening to binaural beats for your entire workday, though, or its effectiveness will diminish.

There is a range of apps available with binaural beats. However, be aware of apps that superimpose binaural beats over rain or ocean sounds – they have actually been shown to have a detrimental impact on learning and focus because they overload the auditory system.

Summary

1. Plan your workday.
2. Snack (don't nibble) on your inbox.
3. Wear noise-cancelling headphones.

PILLAR III

DISABLE DIGITAL DISTRACTIONS

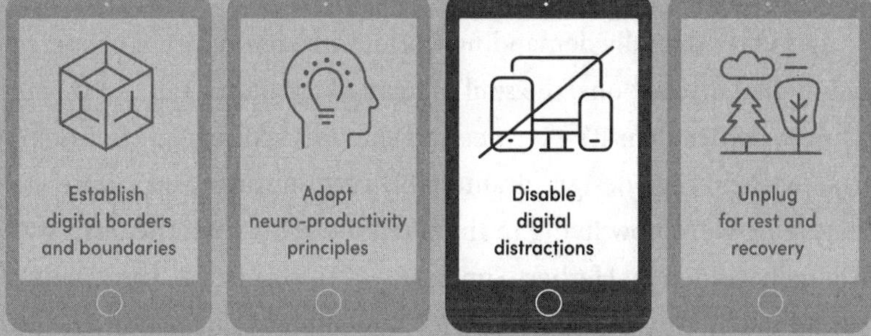

As a working mum, Bec was racing to the shops on a wet Monday morning to grab some lunchbox supplies. She was juggling the grocery bag on one arm and clutching her phone with her other hand when she received a phone call. She took the call on her headphones and was chatting to her colleague when tragedy struck: distracted, she walked out onto the road and was hit by a truck. Bec died at the scene, leaving behind a husband and two young children.

Sadly, this story is not uncommon. A 2019 paper by NRMA reported that increasing numbers of people are now 'smombies' (smartphone zombies) when they're pedestrians, so distracted by their phones or headphones that their safety is compromised. The harsh reality is that digital distractions can be deadly.

In aviation there's something called the 'sterile cockpit rule'. (I'm so grateful for this rule as I sit here writing this, ironically, on a plane.) This is a procedural requirement that strictly prohibits pilots and cabin crew from being distracted by non-essential activities in the cockpit during critical phases of the flight, which is typically when the plane is involved in taxi, take-off, landing and when the plane is at a height of less than 10,000 feet. This rule was imposed in 1981 after it was discovered that several accidents were caused by pilots and cabin crew being distracted from their flying duties by engaging in irrelevant conversations and activities during critical stages of the flight. This highlights what many of us intuitively know: when we need to do focused, mentally taxing work, we need to eliminate as many distractions as possible.

In today's digitally demanding world, when our days are peppered with digital distractions, the skill of focused attention is under threat. It's now harder than it's ever been to stay focused. Digital technologies, by their very design, drain and divert our attention. Some are suggesting we're now living in the 'attention economy'. The term was originally coined by Herbert Simon in 1971 (long before the internet was adopted). Simon suggested that 'a wealth of information creates a poverty of attention and a need to allocate that attention efficiently among the overabundance of information sources that might consume it'. The term has also become popularised in recent times by Google's former design ethicist Tristan Harris, who talked about it in his TED talk and in *The Social Dilemma*.

Therefore, I believe that the super skill we all need to cultivate is focus. While we've long known that high performance is often determined by a person's combined IQ (their general intelligence) and EQ (emotional intelligence), I believe a skill that's more important than both of those skills combined is our FQ (focus quotient).

Focused attention is the chief super skill of the 21st century. It determines how effectively you can sustain your focus. 'Focus is the engine room of knowledge work', according to Michael Gold from the Economist Intelligence Unit. And, yes, I have a quick online tool you can use to determine your FQ, which can be accessed via the Book Resources page of my website.

As the digital intensity of our days has increased exponentially in recent years, so too has our propensity to be distracted. Studies suggest that adults pick up their smartphones an average of 96 times per day, which equates to about once every ten minutes. (I shudder to think what our screenagers' daily pick-up rates would be.) We're tethered to technology and so easily distracted by alerts and notifications that having time to engage in sustained focused work seems to be a relic from the past. Therefore, it's paramount that we learn to better manage one of the chief culprits that hijacks our attention: digital distraction.

It's time for you to win the war for your attention by applying brain-based strategies to tame your tech habits! Pillar III has three practices that will equip you with realistic, research-based strategies to take back control and stop technology distracting you:

1. Manage your digital load.
2. Create more friction.
3. Minimise your tech temptations.

Practice 7

Manage your digital load

Humans are biologically designed to go and seek information at a time, cadence and volume that suits us. We're information gatherers. However, today, information is constantly being thrust at us. It's hard to resist and it's easy to quickly become distracted by it.

Digital micro-stressors trigger your nervous system. Your brain perceives these external signals – pings, vibrations, alerts – as a threat. Remember, your brain cannot differentiate between a tiger chasing you and a Teams notification: they're both perceived as threats.

Your brain works in concert with your endocrine system (which regulates your hormones) to flood your body with chemicals such as epinephrine (also known as adrenaline), norepinephrine and cortisol and create a variety of physiological responses. Your blood pressure soars, your heart rate accelerates and your fight, flight or freeze response (your sympathetic nervous system) is activated. Your senses are refined, too: your vision is primed to search for escape routes and your hearing to listen out for other potential predators. This physiological response occurs every time we hear a ping from one of our devices.

In this practice, I share three micro-habits that will help you to take back control of your digital devices – realistic strategies that you can apply so you're no longer a slave to the screen.

Micro-habit 1: Activate Do Not Disturb mode

I've mentioned previously that one of our most basic psychological drivers is the need for relational connection. We're biologically wired to want to feel like we're part of a tribe. This is why it's nearly impossible for some of us to go on holidays 'laptopless' and refrain from checking our emails. It's why it can be so hard to ignore the Teams chat notifications that illuminate our phones at 11 p.m. on a Wednesday.

I often say, 'The basics work if you work the basics'. One of the easiest things that we can do to stop digital distractions from diverting our attention is to activate Do Not Disturb (DND) mode (which can sometimes be called Focus mode). You can now activate DND mode on your smartphone, on communication channels like Slack and Teams, and even in your inbox (with some email hosts).

These features are evolving. You can now synchronise your phone with your calendar, so if you have events in your calendar marked as 'work' or 'meetings', or even 'date night', it can automatically activate DND mode. Now there's no excuse for checking your phone during a meeting, or when you're out to dinner with your partner.

You can also customise your DND mode by creating rules and exceptions. For example, if you have elderly parents or young children, or you're working with a colleague on a time-sensitive task, you can have a rule that says to block all calls and notifications between 8:30 a.m. and 1 p.m. with the exception of those from people who may need to contact you urgently. This allows you to have far fewer distractions vying for your attention while also giving you peace of mind knowing that important calls or messages will get through.

These are my top tips for activating DND mode.

Mute notifications on communication tools

Each platform has different configurations, but most apps and web-based tools have a DND (or Focus) mode. For example, in Slack and

Teams, your colleagues can still send you messages, but you won't receive notifications during your nominated DND periods.

Some platforms also now allow users to override DND if something is of critical importance. These need to be legitimately urgent situations, not just someone wanting a quick reply. Otherwise, the DND override function will be a bit like the boy who cried wolf: people will ignore the messages if they don't think they're important.

Set up DND mode on your phone

DND (or Focus) mode blocks notifications from specific apps. It also prohibits you from opening specific apps that you've nominated in your settings during specified hours. Determine which calendar events you want to automatically activate DND mode for.

Do the same for your laptop or desktop

Many of us active DND mode on our phones but overlook our desktops and laptops, which can sometimes have just as many distractions – if not more these days, given the plethora of workplace communication tools we now rely on with hybrid work. Don't forget to activate DND mode on your laptop or desktop as well.

Micro-habit 2: Manage your notifications

Notifications are a distraction disaster. Whether you're out socialising with friends, having a conversation with your partner or doing some deep work, a ping on your phone can destroy the moment. You've probably had that sinking feeling when you're having dinner with a loved one, you get a notification on your phone and you glance down: 'Arrgh! A client is emailing me on a Friday after 7 p.m., so it must be a major problem,' you tell yourself as you excuse yourself to tend to the email, while your loved one sits there, frustrated that once again you've been yanked back to work by your phone. Your heart rate accelerates, cortisol floods your body and panic sets in because the client email is terse and aggressive. That cherished moment with your loved one is annihilated. You return to the table and apologise, but your mind is elsewhere. The night is ruined.

It's not just our work and personal notifications that are pervasive today; notifications are no longer confined to simply emails and SMS pings. We also receive notifications about bill payments, reminders about doctor's appointments, updates about online shopping deliveries (giving us a blow-by-blow of where our package is) and confirmations of online banking transactions. Pings and dings have become the soundtrack of modern-day life. They are a constant sensory assault, as these notifications often flash and vibrate as well as ping. Once again, this overloads our sensory and nervous systems, putting us in an elevated stress state. No wonder so many of us feel OUSTED.

The problem with notifications is that they come to us. This tricks our brains into thinking that they're urgent and important, because our brains are biologically wired to perceive external and unsolicited sounds, colours and movements as possible threats. Further, like well-trained puppies, our devices have conditioned us to react to these notifications: while most notifications are boring, irrelevant or redundant, *occasionally* we receive an exciting, high-reward notification (like an update on a delivery, a sweet message from your partner or some praise from your leader). This creates a Pavlovian response; we tell ourselves, 'This might be an exciting/important/good one', and so we want to check it straight away. This results in a hit of dopamine, which overrides the prefrontal cortex that would otherwise encourage us to resist the urge of picking up our phone.

Studies have shown that simply receiving a push notification is as distracting as responding to a text message or a phone call. Even if you resist the urge to open the notification and read it in its entirety, just glancing at the sender and the truncated view of the message can be distracting. Momentarily transitioning between your current context and the notification causes you to leave behind what Professor Sophie Leroy calls 'attention residue'. Even if you think that quickly checking a notification and then batting it away so you can return to the work you were doing (or the conversation you were having) is the best option, it's cognitively taxing. You leave behind fragments of your attention on the notification. You start to ponder if your colleague was messaging you to compliment you or to complain. It's then hard to get your momentum back. As you may recall from Practice 6, it takes around 23 minutes to get back into a deep, focused state after a digital intruder has fractured your attention. So, even a quick glance that takes just a couple of seconds can be deadly to your performance.

The onus is on you to take the time to manage your notifications. Here are my golden rules for doing this.

Prune your non-essential notifications

When you buy a new device or download a new app, it will immediately start firing off notifications by default, because developers know this is a guaranteed way to get you to spend more time on their platforms. You probably hear the cacophony of notification sounds in your office throughout the day.

Do you really need to be notified that an old colleague just got promoted, via her humble-brag LinkedIn post? No. Go to your settings and disable any non-essential notifications. You'll need to do this on your phone *and* desktop for some apps. You may decide that you don't want any alerts from specific platforms, so ensure that these notifications are completely disabled. Removing the notification bubble that declares how many messages you haven't yet read will reduce your distractions. (It's no accident that the notification bubble is red: red is a psychological trigger for urgency and importance, and the number inside the bubble drives you to open it.)

Batch or bundle your notifications

Rather than having digital intruders trickle in throughout the day, you can now nominate what time/s of the day you'd like to receive specific notifications. Referred to as 'bundling', 'batching' or 'grouped notifications', this capability allows you to take back control of *when* notifications come to you.

For example, I'm a lion and do my deep, focused work in the morning, so I bundle my Slack notifications for between 2 and 3 p.m., when I do my shallow work. I can't stand the constant barrage of WhatsApp notifications from the parent groups I'm part of for my three sons and their various school and sport groups, so when I'm really needing to focus, I'll elect to bundle WhatsApp notifications for 8 p.m. I have a friend who serves as a gatekeeper in the various WhatsApp groups and sends me an SMS if there are any time-critical or urgent messages in each group. (She calls herself the 'watchdog'.) Unsurprisingly, there's rarely anything that's urgent or important enough for her to send to me.

Create VIP notifications

I think we can all agree that email notifications are a productivity killer. A gentle reminder: if you haven't turned off your email notifications, please do so pronto. In fact, I believe it's so essential that I want you to put this book down and go do it immediately. Just don't get so distracted by your bulging inbox that you forget to come back here!

However, I understand that sometimes you might be working on a project with a tight deadline or dealing with a serious issue, and time-sensitive information may need to be shared with you by specific team members or clients. This is where VIP mail notifications can be a game changer. On most email providers, you can elevate specific senders to VIP status and receive notifications each time they send you an email, while everyone else is blocked. This allows you to tackle your deep work with full assurance that you'll only be notified about those essential emails.

Mute conversations or chats

I've been in one too many WhatsApp groups or Slack channels where people reply to one message using a thumbs up or 'thanks' when no reply was necessary. This is often the case if you're in a large group to discuss a project. The mute option is a sanity saver on these occasions. To tame your digital intruders, mute notifications for the time that you require. Don't worry, you'll still see the messages; you just won't be alerted every single time someone replies in these threads.

Micro-habit 3: Disable auto-play

If you've got children or teens, chances are you've endured a techno-tantrum: you've asked them to switch off the TV or iPad (or any digital device, really) and they emotionally combust. Yet again, screen time ends in scream time – from them and you!

One of the reasons that kids and teens find it so challenging to switch off devices is that they feel like they're not finished. The online world is a bottomless bowl; there's *always* another YouTube clip, another message they need to send or receive, or another level in the game. In the absence of stopping cues, they enter the 'state of insufficiency'. This is why they look at you with their puppy-dog eyes and plead desperately, 'Just five more minutes… puh-lease?' And the recommendation algorithms know exactly what video or social media post to serve up next. It's a vicious cycle.

While we know as adults that it's socially inappropriate to combust when we need to switch off our devices, if we're honest, we also struggle with the state of insufficiency. We find it hard to switch off. We strive but fail to ever reach inbox zero. We keep doomscrolling social media on the bus on the way home, instead of using the time to close our eyes and decompress. We binge-watch TV when we really should be in bed. In Lisa Corduff's study mentioned in the introduction to this book, 50 per cent of respondents said that the worst thing about their screen habits was their inability to manage their time online. No wonder so many of us feel OUSTED: our tech habits have taken hold of us and are robbing us of our time and attention.

The auto-play feature is one of the reasons we can't stop. Auto-play is now the default setting for most online video streaming services, such as YouTube and Netflix, as well as for videos in your social media feeds. This allows videos to keep playing back to back without requiring any activation from the user. No wonder so many of us can easily binge-watch an entire Netflix series or suffer from revenge bedtime procrastination at night. Why do tech companies do this? The reason is simple: to make you spend longer on the platform. A Deloitte survey found that the average Australian user of streaming services consumes three or more episodes per sitting, so it's clear that the auto-play feature works. Netflix CEO Reed Hastings once boldly declared that Netflix's biggest competitor was sleep! It's well established in the research and from personal experience that the auto-play feature drags us into a procrastination phase.

Manage auto-play settings

Here's how to disable the auto-play feature. Go to each platform's settings and turn off the auto-play option. You'll need to repeat this process for all social media platforms and video streaming services. Some apps make this much harder than others, but activating the 'data save' mode can sometimes restrict videos from being auto-played.

Check when you update

Unfortunately, sometimes when you update an app it will 'conveniently' re-enable the auto-play feature. Be mindful that you may need to frequently check the auto-play feature is disabled.

Summary

1. Activate Do Not Disturb mode.
2. Manage notifications.
3. Disable auto-play.

Practice 8

Create more friction

You pull out your phone and order a ride. You're informed who will drive you, their vehicle model and precisely what time they'll arrive to collect you. You can watch the driver approaching (and, often, you can see them sitting in traffic). You pay for the ride without ever pulling out your wallet or credit card, and a receipt is sent straight to your inbox.

Easy-peasy. There's no long wait on a phone while you listen to horrendous on-hold music; no trying to hail a cab in the rain; no repeating your current location and destination over and over; no getting in a taxi and having the driver refuse to drive you to your destination; and no fee blowouts because the traffic is at a standstill. An Uber ride is far more efficient and often (but not always) more affordable than a taxi.

If there's one thing companies like Meta (formerly Facebook), Uber, Amazon and Apple have in common (besides mind-boggling profits), it is that they've created *frictionless* experiences for users. Tech companies have recognised, in their relentless pursuit to dominate our attention, that removing any barriers that act as extra or onerous steps users must undergo to access a service has made their technologies easier than ever to use. YouTube even has a premium offering, meaning you can watch the same content minus the advertisements if you pay for a subscription.

Would you feel compelled to check your emails or social media notifications if the notification bubble was mint green or sky blue? Probably not. One of the reasons we often get lured into the digital rabbit hole is the use of colours on our screen. Human eyes are sensitive to warm colours. Eye-tracking tests show that the human eye is drawn to bright colours, especially red. Red is a psychological trigger for danger, urgency and importance; this is why many emergency vehicles and lifeguard services use red. It is also why many social media companies have recently updated their icons to brighter and bolder colours, and why our notification bubbles are usually red: they draw us in.

Another way that our devices lure us in is via metrics. Metrics now permeate our digital world, such as in the form of those little red notification bubbles boldly declaring that we have 48 unread emails, 57 Teams chat notifications and 18 text messages left unread. Metrics act as a very tangible reminder of outstanding tasks and compel us to keep checking and using our electronic devices. We look for the quick wins and get hooked into completing shallow, easy tasks, such as reading our emails so we can reduce 48 down to ten (and zero would make us feel even better, as many email providers now provide us with a congratulatory message if we reach inbox zero to celebrate a fleeting moment in time). This, in turn, contributes to overwhelm, because we know we're not spending time on the tasks that require more of our focus and would yield the best results – and this further compromises our capacity to pay attention. It's a vicious cycle we can get trapped in.

Another reason we can so easily get drawn into the digital vortex is completion bias. Basically, we're biologically wired to complete tasks because of the perceived pleasure we anticipate it will bring. We all feel good when we finish a task; there's a sense of feeling 'done'.

Studies have confirmed what many of us intuitively know: that checking off items from our to-do list is psychologically rewarding. Whenever we cross something off our list, our brain releases a small hit of dopamine, the pleasure neurotransmitter that drives our reward-motivated behaviours; this naturally makes us want to finish more tasks and cross more off our to-do lists. Surely I'm not the only one who occasionally writes tasks on my to-do list for the simple pleasure I know I'll derive from crossing them off?

I'm sure we've all had moments when we open our laptops to send just *one* client email, but before we know it our attention has been derailed by a multitude of not-very-important emails flooding our inbox. So, let's look at some realistic strategies we can apply to our digital technologies to add back some more friction so we're less likely to slip down the digital black hole.

Micro-habit 1: Out of sight, out of mind

The first strategy is that adage your mum probably said to you: 'Out of sight, out of mind.' The research is compelling when it comes to your phone being a source of distraction: just seeing your phone can be a mental brain drain. Research from the University of Texas at Austin confirmed that when you're working with your phone in your line of sight, it reduces your cognitive performance, even if it's on silent and in Do Not Disturb mode. Put simply, seeing your phone makes you dumber! Your phone is literally a brain drain.

These are my top tips for removing your tech temptations from your line of sight.

Put your phone out of sight when doing deep work

Put your phone in a drawer or in another room, or leave it in your bag, when you need to do deep, focused work. I've had timber charging boxes designed so you can easily tuck your phone away and charge it while you do your deep work.

Put your laptop or tablet away at the end of the workday

One of the reasons so many of us slip down the digital rabbit hole after hours is because we see our devices sitting on the dining table or the lounge. This visual cue can be enough to make us start ruminating about work, and so we eventually pull out our laptop. Putting your device somewhere where you cannot see it can remove this visual cue. If you're a parent, you may want to consider using a metallic charging box from Inchargebox to store laptops, tablets and phones at night.

Replace your tech temptation with another visual cue

Want to start walking at night instead of binge-watching Netflix? Put your sneakers near where the TV remote typically sits. Want to stop scrolling social media at night and read a book instead? Put a book next to your bed and keep your phone out of your room. In his book *Atomic Habits*, James Clear proposes that these visual cues nudge us to adopt healthier habits.

Micro-habit 2: Log out

I don't know about you, but I have trouble remembering the 721 different passwords I have for various apps and websites. I'm not the only one: studies confirm that many of us are suffering from 'digital dementia' these days. Put simply, because of the constant onslaught of information you're being exposed to each day in the online world, your brain's hippocampus (the memory centre) cannot cope. You may recall (or possibly not recall) from the introduction to this book that many of us are suffering from infobesity as we're being constantly bombarded with digital information. The result? We just can't seem to remember things like we once did. Can you recall more than three phone numbers these days? If so, are they numbers you memorised from years ago?

A simple strategy to tackle the frictionless experience that digital technologies offer us is to log out of the various apps and websites that are your tech temptations. Why? Because, when you want to use the app or website again, you'll need to log back in. This creates an intermediary step that will either frustrate you (as you try the various passwords you've used over the years: was it your mother's maiden name, your son's birth date or your husband's nickname?) or simply create an extra step that can make you pause momentarily and nudge you to do something else.

Given that our memory skills have declined, many of us will be unlikely to recall the password. Sure, we can reset the password, or attempt to answer the security questions we set up when we first made the account years ago; but these steps add friction, which may deter us from using the app or website.

Here are my top tips to nudge you to log off.

Logging out rules

I've worked with some executives who know that they won't resist the lure of their inboxes over the weekend. To combat this, they have their EA reset their passwords on Friday afternoon so that they cannot do a sneaky email check over the weekend. Their EA then resets the password on Monday morning. Now, of course, this may not be feasible all the time (and many of us don't have an EA): there will certainly be occasions when you legitimately need to email over the weekend, or at least when you'd feel better drafting and scheduling emails over the weekend. You could perhaps create your own logout rules such as, 'I'm going to log out of emails on Friday at 5 p.m. and not open them again until Monday at 8 a.m.'

Log out of social media accounts

If you're lured by LinkedIn or intrigued by Instagram, try logging out of these apps. Every time you want to use them, you'll need to recall or reset your password, both of which are time-consuming and so may deter you from using the apps.

Log out and change your password

Use a password tool that can only be accessed on a desktop computer, such as LastPass. (While most of these tools have an app version, just sticking to the desktop version means you're less likely to use the app on your phone.) This strategy has dual benefits: it will create more friction, because you'll only be able to log on via a computer (our phones really are frictionless); and you'll free up some of your cognitive resources, because you won't need to remember the password.

Shut down your devices

By turning off our phones, laptops and desktops, we create more friction, because there are extra steps required to turn them back on; this may deter us from using them. Now, I'm not talking about locking your phone, or putting your device in sleep mode: I'm talking about a full shut down. Not only will it deter your usage, but it can also make your machine run a lot faster after it's been restarted.

Micro-habit 3: Use tech-prohibition tools

You've got a looming deadline for an important report. You know you just need to spend the day uninterrupted to get it done, so you've decided to work from home. You make a great start, but then your Teams chat starts pinging and there's a cacophony of WhatsApp notifications on your phone from a work colleague requiring urgent information. So, you go into your inbox intending to send just one email to your colleague but, before you know it, you're triaging your emails. This can so easily happen.

If you've tried the other two micro-habits in this practice and still find yourself here, then perhaps you need a more stringent approach. The third micro-habit I suggest is to outsource your willpower by using a tech tool that will prohibit you from using certain apps or platforms at set times of the day. The reason we can't rely on willpower alone is because it naturally depletes with each temptation we must resist over the day. The prefrontal cortex, which is the chief brain region involved in resisting tech urges, becomes exhausted.

Think of your willpower like a glass of water. You start with a full cup. For every decision you make, you take a sip from your cup. Just as your cup will empty as you take more sips from it, so too will your willpower!

Every email you open (or ignore), every SMS that you read (or disregard), every link you click on (or decide not to click on) depletes your willpower. Trying to resist your tech temptations all day is like trying to run up a steep, muddy hill: it's exhausting and plain hard. Yet, many of us spend our days relying on our willpower to help us resist our digital urges. Given what we now know about some of the persuasive techniques that tech companies use to hijack our attention, perhaps we should look for alternatives to our willpower to resist digital distractions.

There is a range of tech tools that can restrict what you access on certain devices. Let's have a look at some of the more common ones available.

Screen Time or Digital Wellbeing features

Use the generic built-in tools that come with most Apple and Android phones today to help you monitor and manage the time you're spending on your phone. If you've ever been brave enough to look at your weekly Screen Time report (for iOS users) or Digital Wellbeing report (for Android users), the average number of hours per day spent on your phone can be sobering (speaking from experience here). With these tools, you can set daily limits and reminders about how much time you want to spend on specific apps.

Now, I know these restrictions are very easy to override, but seeing a reminder that you've hit your daily Instagram limit by 8 a.m. can be enough of a psychological nudge for you to re-evaluate your digital habits.

Freedom

Freedom is an app and website blocker for Mac, Windows, iOS, Android and Chrome. You can use this tool to block distractions so you can accomplish your focused work. Block what you want when you want to focus and be more productive. You can establish focus time on the fly or schedule it in advance.

RescueTime

RescueTime is a web-based time management tool that allows you to specify focus-work goals and keeps track of what you're doing on your computer. This tool automatically tracks your time online, knows what you're working on and alerts you to your most productive times, highlights what distracts you and reports on how well you focus.

Confession: I installed this tool and was expecting a glowing report. I opened my first weekly report and metric dashboard and almost fell off my chair when I learned that I'd spent 31 per cent of my week on emails! I totally overhauled my inbox habits after this.

Inbox When Ready

This is a Gmail browser extension that helps you check your inbox frequently, batch-process emails on a regular schedule and minimise the time you're spending in your inbox. You can set a lockout schedule and specify how many minutes you'd like to dedicate to email each day to help you adhere to your deep-focused work schedule. Then, you simply go in and batch-process your emails at the best time of day for you. You get real-time feedback comparing your intention to your actual usage, so it can nudge you to adopt better habits.

Summary

1. Out of sight, out of mind.
2. Log out.
3. Try tech-prohibition tools.

Practice 9

Minimise your tech temptations

I'll admit I was horrified when I received my first Screen Time report and saw just how many hours I'd squandered on my phone: an average of five hours a day! I tried to rationalise the number by convincing myself that a lot of that time was 'work', but the harsh reality was that a significant amount of it was leisure. Have you checked your Screen Time (iOS) or Digital Wellbeing (Android) report?

Some experts are suggesting that our phones are making us 'dopamine junkies', and each swipe, like and comment is fuelling our dirty digital habit. Dr Anna Lembke, in her book *Dopamine Nation*, suggests that the smartphone is the 'modern-day hypodermic needle'. While I think this claim is a little alarmist and suggests that psychological addictions are akin to substance addictions, I do believe that many of us have some unhealthy digital dependencies and habits, especially when it comes to our phones.

We self-soothe with our screens and placate ourselves for hours on our phones, turning to them for quick hits, distraction and validation. The online world is like a sensory smorgasbord offering us endless opportunities to be stimulated, satiated or seduced, whether we enter the Instagram vortex, swipe through Tinder, shop online, binge on Netflix or gamble our time away. We now have portals of pleasure at the tip of our fingers, requiring minimal cognitive effort.

It's important to note that research is still in its infancy in this space, and that there are both positive and negative impacts associated with how our brains are being shaped and influenced by technology. However, what we do know is that, when faced with the decision to complete complex data analysis or check email, the striatum (a part of the brain that's integral to our reward system) will urge us to take the 'easy route' and jump into our inboxes. In turn, dopamine hijacks the frontal lobe of the brain that would otherwise regulate our behaviour. Therefore, getting stuck in Slack or constantly nibbling at emails throughout the day can become habitual patterns because of the constant digital dopamine dump. (This also explains why we might start off with the intention of eating one square of chocolate, but one can quickly become two, which then becomes half the block...)

Many of us are now spending more time with pixels than people, especially as we shift to remote and hybrid work arrangements and rely on digital communications more than ever. Many of us believe that our online interactions with friends and family are an ample substitute because they're quick and easy. However, while digital communication tools and social media are great ways to share information, research has shown that in-person interactions are far superior in terms of reducing cortisol levels and strengthening our bonds with others. When we interact with people in close physical proximity, our brains release a hormone called 'oxytocin'; sometimes referred to as the 'love hormone' or 'social bonding hormone', it strengthens our bonds with others and reduces our stress and anxiety. Unfortunately, online interactions do not biochemically replicate our in-person connections.

Scanning and searching for new, interesting or unusual sights, sounds or smells has helped us to evolve as a species (so we could look and listen for impending threats or dangers). The problem is that today, the online world is like a sensory smorgasbord: we have so many sensory inputs vying for our attention that our brain doesn't know how to distinguish between critical information and superfluous, irrelevant information. The online world is *always* interesting, exciting and easy – we don't have to exert too much cognitive effort to watch our favourite TV show or scroll through LinkedIn. If it isn't new or exciting then we can simply change channels or close the app and open a new one. The offline, analog world is slow-paced and monotonous by comparison and requires significant cognitive effort at times.

So, let's now look at ways we can arm ourselves with the habits that make our digital devices less tempting.

Micro-habit 1: Go greyscale

When Steve Jobs released the first iPod touch, he said that he had designers make the app icons so physiologically appealing that users would want to lick their screens. Yes, lick their screens! This tells us a lot about the persuasive and clever use of colour, as we discussed in the previous practice.

So, a simple yet powerful technique is to go to your device's settings and turn it to greyscale. This turns your colourful display monochrome and basically makes your device more drab and less fun. I'll vouch that Instagram is *very* boring in black and white. This feature is available on both iOS and Android devices and is free to use. (A quick Google search should yield you simple step-by-step instructions on how to activate greyscale on your device and operating system.)

According to Tristan Harris, greyscale removes the positive reinforcements that colours offer our brains, as our eyes are biologically designed to be attracted to bright and shiny objects. In turn, it's believed that greyscale dampens our urge to touch our phones and lure us to spend more time online.

The bright red notification bubbles boldly declaring that you have 17 unread text messages, or 28 WhatsApp messages, or 123 unopened emails, appear much less aggressive and tempting when they've been changed to a dull grey colour. While they're still legible, they don't appear to be shouting at you and demanding your attention.

So, how can you make the most of greyscale mode?

Determine when you're most likely to be distracted by your phone

Perhaps you're a late-night social media doomscroller. Maybe you know you just can't resist the urge to pick up your phone at your son's swimming lesson. Perhaps there's a tight deadline on a work project, and you know that you'll reach for your phone when you hit a challenging task. These are the times of the day when you may benefit from enabling greyscale.

Quickly activate greyscale mode

There is an array of phone and tablet shortcuts that allow you to quickly activate greyscale mode. If it's too convoluted to set up, this won't be a tech habit that sticks. I've managed to adjust my settings so that a triple click of my phone's side button instantly activates greyscale mode (and the same shortcut also reverts it to colour when required). Can you make a similar shortcut?

Micro-habit 2: Maximise your windows

For similar reasons that we may want to turn our phones to greyscale, maximising our laptop or desktop computer's windows can also be an effective way to become less distracted by our digital devices.

Let's say you're working on a report in a Word document. You really need to be focused and eliminate as many distractions as possible. By maximising your Word window, you're much less likely to dive into your internet browser or your inbox when you hit a challenging part of your report. If the appealing icons or tabs are not visible, you're much less likely to turn to these tech temptations.

Here are some ways that you can optimise your window view.

Go full-screen mode

Determine the work tasks (or perhaps the tech tools) that warrant your full attention. For me, I know that when I'm doing data analysis in Excel I must go to full-screen mode. Inputting complex formulae or interpreting results in a spreadsheet is demanding, so I know I'm likely to hit a challenging component in Excel and risk succumbing to distraction.

Hide your toolbar

The toolbar or taskbar at the bottom (or sometimes the top or side) of your screen, with its tempting, colourful icons, is another source of distraction – especially when you need to do your deep work. So, go to your computer's settings and find out how you can hide it.

Close all tabs

Having 17 tabs open on your web browser at once can be distracting, not to mention mentally draining. Remember, your eyes are receiving around 10 million pieces of information every second, so seeing these additional 16 tabs places unnecessary demands on your attention. Close all tabs apart from the one (or perhaps two or three) that you need open to perform your current task.

You can close the unrequired tabs manually, or you can use a browser extension that does this for you. I use the Close All Tabs extension for Chrome. Now, before you panic at 'losing' all your open tabs, consider using a system for saving and managing your favourite websites. I use Evernote and Pocket for saving websites and archiving articles, videos or podcasts I want to consume.

Having just one tab open at a time will not only make you less vulnerable to distractions, but it will make your computer run a whole lot more efficiently, too.

Micro-habit 3: Hide your tech temptations

Previously, we explored the idea of putting phones out of sight when we need to do deep, focused work. That's also a relevant strategy for minimising tech temptations. However, I want to get a little more granular and suggest that we find other ways to make our phones and other digital devices less enticing. Our devices are too frictionless and fun, so we need to take deliberate actions to add greater friction to use them and make them less appealing.

Here are my top tips for hiding your tech temptations.

Delete troublesome apps off your phone

If you can't resist checking LinkedIn or your football app when you really should be writing your annual report, consider deleting the app off your device. This doesn't mean deleting your account, of course. Instead, make a pact to check the app only on your laptop or desktop computer. This means that you're much more intentional about how and when you use the app (especially if you're using tech prohibition tools on your laptop or desktop computer that quantify your time on various platforms).

Remove your tech temptations off your phone's home screen

Tell me I'm not the only one who does this: I unlock my phone just to send one SMS and before I know it I'm checking LinkedIn, opening

Instagram, checking tomorrow's weather, replying to three-day-old WhatsApp messages and quickly scanning my inbox. Why? Because these app icons are all on the home page of my phone.

I've now moved my tech temptations (Instagram, LinkedIn and Facebook, I'm talking about you) off my home screen and tucked them in an obscure location on the fifth screen on my phone. Hugh van Cuylenburg, author of *The Resilience Project*, suggests taking this a step further and dragging your tech-temptation icons into a folder called 'Things I'll Later Regret', so that every time you open them, you're hit with a pang of guilt.

Keep only functional apps on your phone's home screen

The home screen on your phone is prime real estate: it's usually the first thing that you see when you unlock your phone. So, seeing Facebook or a news app when you first unlock your phone can lure you down a digital rabbit hole. Keeping only functional apps on your phone's home screen can prevent this.

Remove tech temptations from your toolbar

The icons on your laptop or desktop can also suck you into the digital vortex, especially when you need to be tackling your deep work. To counteract this, delete the icons for digital weakness from the toolbar. You'll still be able to access them, but you'll have to go to your application window to launch them. Again, the purpose of this is to create more intermediary steps to deter you from getting distracted.

Summary

1. Go greyscale.
2. Maximise your windows.
3. Hide your tech temptations.

PILLAR IV

UNPLUG FOR REST AND RECOVERY

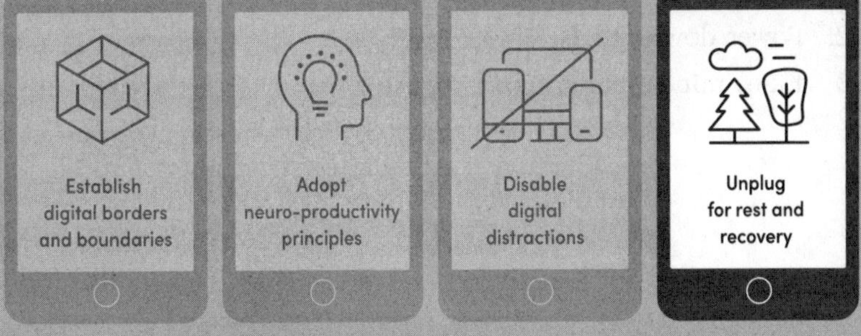

Maybe you tell yourself it's 'just a busy period at work'. Maybe it's the end of financial year, or perhaps you've been swamped with a massive project at work, or maybe you've just started a new role. The thing is, we trick ourselves into believing that if we can get just 'one more thing' done, life will feel more manageable or like it's at a more palatable pace. Just one more email, one more meeting, one more SMS, one more social media post, one more project. Just one more thing.

However, the fatigue is relentless. Your morning coffee no longer does the trick and you convince yourself that you'll feel better if you can just catch up on some extra sleep over the weekend. Monday arrives, you're still exhausted and the pressures of your world shout – loudly.

Regardless of which stage of stress you're at, there are simple, attainable things you can do to recover and strategies you can put in place to tackle burnout.

One of the most vital things that we can do to tackle and stop the OUSTED cycle many of us are trapped in is to take regular breaks and digitally disconnect. Coupled with manageable workloads, intentionally pausing to recover is fundamental to thriving in the digital world. We need to be deliberate about unplugging.

Pillar IV examines why rest and recuperation are paramount in stopping us from being stuck in an OUSTED cycle and, in fact, proposes that rest is a critical component of peak performance in a digital age. You can achieve this through the following practices:

1. Peak-performance pit stops.
2. Power-down rituals.
3. Enjoy mind-wandering.

Practice 10

Take peak-performance pit stops

While I'm no motor racing fan, I've always been fascinated by what happens during pit stops. They're frenetic and precisely executed, and there are dire consequences if they're skipped. This has led me to ponder, why do racing drivers take pit stops? Why, in one of the most high-stakes race formats in the world, do they spend precious time refuelling, changing tyres, performing repairs and making mechanical adjustments? Surely these supreme vehicles and well-trained drivers can finish the race without a pit stop?

It turns out that these pit stops are integral to a motor racing team's success. According to IndyCar Series driver Will Power, 'A lot of races are won in the pit'. These supreme vehicles are under enormous stress, so pit stops help them to optimise their performance and identify issues early. They also allow them to refuel, because even the best vehicles can't run on empty.

As knowledge workers, we need to act like racing drivers – who also strive for peak performance – by taking regular pit stops. If you want to thrive in the digital world, you need to be intentional about taking breaks.

We need to shift the dialogue around rest so that we don't consider it lazy. Rest isn't something that we get around to at 5 p.m. on Sunday when we've *finally* ticked everything off our to-do list, nor is it something that we should just reserve for our annual leave. We really must redefine rest as something that's fundamental to peak performance. We can rest and still achieve peak performance; they're not diametrically opposed. In fact, I'd go as far as to say that we *must* rest to achieve peak performance.

We factor in time for machines to undergo maintenance. We take our cars to get serviced. We charge our laptops. We update our phones' operating systems. We do all these things to improve our machines' performance. So, why don't we do the same for ourselves?

Research tells us that many of us are working longer hours. This is eroding the time we once had for rest and recovery. Studies disagree over just how much longer our workdays have become since shifting to hybrid work, but they unanimously agree that there's been an increase. One study by Qatalog and GitLab found that knowledge workers were spending an additional 67 minutes each day attempting to prove that they're online and not slacking off, a trend called 'digital presenteeism'. It appears that we've absorbed the commute we once had into work time.

However, working long hours can be seriously detrimental to our health – in fact, it can literally kill us. Research conducted by the World Health Organization and International Labour Organization showed that working more than 55 hours per week led to 745,000 deaths from stroke and heart disease in 2016 – a 29 per cent increase since 2000 when similar data was collected. Yet, this has become the operating cadence many people, especially knowledge workers, are adopting.

Since the shift towards remote work, many people are finding it even more challenging to switch off from work, physically and psychologically. Our reliance on digital technologies as we embrace remote and hybrid work means that it's more likely we'll fatigue, with studies confirming what many of us have intuitively known: that working on screens is exhausting (hello Zoom fatigue, digital eye strain and tech neck).

If we want to tackle burnout, then we must manage stress and catch stress at its early stages. A 2021 study confirmed that 71 per cent of Americans feel tense or stressed at work. We have to stop the depletion spiral many people are facing and the best way to do this is to take intentional rest periods. We need to invest in our rest.

Studies have shown that a psychological detachment from work can help to bolster wellbeing and engagement. Dr Sahar Yousef suggests a 3M framework to prevent burnout: by taking micro-, meso- and macro-breaks. She asserts that taking regular breaks can help to close the stress cycle and, in doing so, prevent burnout. I like to visualise these breaks like coffee sizes: piccolo, tall and grande.

Micro-habit 1: Take piccolo breaks

Piccolo breaks are typically two to ten minutes in duration and should occur frequently throughout your day. You should be taking four to six piccolo breaks each day while working. They should be short periods of respite. Just like a piccolo coffee, they're small but effective.

Such brief breaks may seem insignificant, but they are incredibly effective. In fact, research by Dr Adam Fraser and Deakin University found that the best way to beat burnout is via short, regular, consistent periods of recovery. Dr Fraser told me:

> 'Our research shows that by far the most common strategy people cited to help them manage burnout was taking a longer break from work in the form of a holiday. Unfortunately, the benefits of a break or holiday have been shown to disappear

three to four weeks after that person returns to work. The most successful model we have found to prevent burnout revolves around getting people to practice short, regular and consistent bursts of recovery. We can no longer rely on holidays to solve our burnout issues; the modern-day worker must learn how to recover on the go.'

Studies have shown that these piccolo breaks yield better results than longer breaks. For example, one study compared the effects of 30 minutes of physical activity performed as one bout in the morning (one 30-minute walk) versus as micro-bouts spread across the day (six five-minute breaks) – with the rest of the day spent sitting – and examined the impact on mood, energy levels and cognitive function. It showed that the micro-bouts and the single long bout both improved energy and vigour, but the micro-bouts also decreased levels of fatigue and food cravings. It also suggested that short bouts of activity during sedentary office workers' days offered a promising approach to enhancing employee wellbeing.

A study involving surgeons showed that taking 20-second breaks every 20 minutes had a positive impact on their physical and mental fatigue. In fact, one study showed that the surgeons were seven times more accurate after they took piccolo breaks and reported experiencing half the level of physical fatigue.

We can use piccolo breaks to implement some practical tools that help us deal with stress. When we increase the biological buffers that help us manage stress, we're likely to reduce our feeling of being OUSTED. These tools can help us to build our stress tolerance, not 'beat' stress. Stress is an inevitable part of being human and there are no known practices that we can implement to make us immune to it – we just need to learn how to dance with stress.

Sophie Scott, an Adjunct Associate Professor at the University of Notre Dame's medical school, says:

> 'Although stress often gets a bad reputation – some levels of stress are quite normal and are in fact good for you – it's important to remember that the purpose of a physiological stress response is to promote survival during flight or fight. In other words, stress in the short-term can be protective and productive, as it prepares your body to face challenges in your everyday life. However, chronic stress can negatively impact the body's immune response. Experiencing chronic stress over a prolonged period raises your cortisol levels, which can weaken your immune system and elevate inflammation, making you more susceptible to viruses and infections.'

Here are some ideas for science-backed piccolo breaks that you can intersperse throughout your day to help you deal with stress.

Close your eyes

As mentioned in Practice 1, closing your eyes, even for just 30 seconds, can be restorative. Your visual system is one of the most energy-intensive functions in your brain. Your occipital lobe, which processes what you see, is easily depleted. You may recall from earlier practices that your eyes are receiving an estimated 10 million pieces of sensory input each second. Closing your eyes gives your occipital lobe a much-needed rest. This technique can take your brain from being in a busy beta state to an alpha, alert, focused state.

Do exhale-emphasised breathing

Yes, your mum was right when she told you to take some deep breaths when you were upset. Breathing activates your parasympathetic nervous system, which is your calming system that helps you manage stress. As mentioned in Practice 2, there is a myriad of breathing techniques, and it really doesn't matter which one you use, so long as your exhalation is longer than your inhalation. Again, only a few cycles need to be performed to have an impact. Best of all, these breathing techniques require no equipment and can be performed anywhere, anytime, even on a Zoom meeting. (Just check you're muted before doing a long exhalation.)

Do rapid, deliberate breathing

I know you're probably thinking, *not another breathing technique*, but hear me out – this is super effective. Made famous by Wim Hof, super-oxygenated breathing speeds up your heart rate, increases adrenaline and puts you in an alert state. Performed for around 15 to 30 cycles, this pattern of breathing involves a series of rapid inhales (through the nose) and exhales (through the mouth), and sounds like a panting dog. The rapid movement of your diaphragm causes blood to flow more slowly through the heart, which drives your brain to send a message to the heart to speed it up, putting you in a focused state. This is an ideal practice to do at the end of your piccolo break to put you in an alert state.

People with anxiety or other mental health issues should take care when performing this exercise as it can make them feel light-headed. Also, for this reason, it should never be performed near water for risk of passing out and drowning.

Hum or sing

Even if performed quietly to yourself, singing or humming creates vibrations that massage a section of your vagus nerve, which is the main nerve of the parasympathetic nervous system. This will quickly calm you down. Like breathing exercises, this can be performed without any apparatus and in a discreet fashion. Adjunct Associate Professor Sophie Scott explains that singing activates your vocal cords, which in turn stimulates the vagus nerve (because it's connected to your vocal cords and the muscles at the back of your throat).

Mammalian diving reflex

When your face is submerged in cold water, your body immediately activates a part of the nervous system that slows everything down. To stimulate your vagus nerve through this technique, Professor Scott recommends that you fill a bowl with ice water or turn on a cold shower and submerge your face in the cold water for at least 15 seconds, then observe your heart rate drop.

Engage in non-sleep deep rest

Professor Andrew Huberman advocates for non-sleep deep rest (NSDR) as an excellent tool that has been shown to put the brain and body in a rested state that mimics sleep in as little as ten minutes. This practice involves lying down and listening to a script that encourages you to scan your body while making long exhalations.

This is not meditation or hypnosis, nor is it a nap. This practice trains your body to activate the parasympathetic nervous system on demand – you are literally training your body to switch to a rested state more efficiently. I often do this in the afternoon as my piccolo break, because it recharges me and allows me to power through the 3 p.m. slump.

Connect and laugh

As simple as it sounds, socialising and laughing with loved ones and colleagues reduces cortisol. Laughter has also been shown to increase heart-rate variability and improve mood. So, can you connect with someone during a piccolo break?

Drink water at your desk

Drinking water at your desk not only hydrates you, which keeps your brain in a prime state, but it also naturally forces you to take a piccolo break to use the bathroom! Simple but effective.

Undertake deliberate cold-exposure protocols

For years, I've loved swimming in the ocean in the middle of winter. Don't get me wrong, I don't love getting *into* the cold water – it's painful, and every part of me screams, 'Kristy, you're mad! Why are you doing this!?' – but I love the feeling when I get out. When I read the science around deliberate cold exposure, I was amazed to learn more about the mechanics behind why it's so effective. Cold exposure helps our body to release epinephrine, norepinephrine and dopamine. These chemicals can improve our cognitive attention, energy and mood, and this explains why our mental state shifts after cold exposure. Studies have shown that there's a 250 to 500 per cent increase in baseline level of these chemicals in our brains after cold exposure.

Now, you probably won't do this practice during the day, but it's an effective micro-habit that you could include as part of your power-up routine at the start of the day. There's science confirming that deliberate exposure to cold can help us manage stress and elevate our focus. We can do this via cold showers, ice baths, ocean swimming in cooler months and going outside without a jumper in winter. The temperature needs to be uncomfortably cold, and exposure should ideally occur at the beginning of the day. The general recommendation is for 11 minutes per week, so that could be three or four three-minute periods each week.

Create a piccolo-break chart

Do you need to power up or power down? Not all piccolo breaks are created the same. Some breaks can give you a boost of energy, while other breaks can calm you down.

Create a T-chart. On the left-hand side, list the piccolo breaks that you can do to power up; on the right-hand side, list the piccolo breaks that you can do to power down. Having a go-to list of what you can do during your break means you don't waste valuable time thinking of what to do, and you're less likely to pick up your phone or check emails instead. Some power-up piccolo breaks include going for a walk, doing lunges or squats, splashing your face with ice-cold water, dancing, listening to music and rapid deliberate breathing. Power-down piccolo breaks may include closing your eyes, exhale-emphasised deep breathing, non-sleep deep rest, lying down, sighing, singing or humming.

Micro-habit 2: Schedule tall breaks

Tall breaks are longer than piccolo breaks and should be performed at least once each day. The minimum effective dose is one to two hours each and every day, but this is an absolute minimum – so if you're doing more than this, that's great.

A tall break should provide *both* a physical and psychological break from your work. It may involve a hobby, a team or individual sport, or some sort of recreational or leisure activity. While it doesn't have to be strictly an organised or regimented commitment, it should be predictable time off, when you can have a break from constantly bashing out work or performing tasks. Just as drinking a tall coffee takes more time than drinking a piccolo coffee, tall breaks require more time than piccolo breaks, but they should also be prioritised each day.

Here are some ideas for managing your tall breaks.

Ring-fence your time

Schedule your tall breaks in your calendar as recurring appointments. This will make you more likely to adhere to them (because let's face it, you're much more likely to do things that you've scheduled in your calendar), and it also stops others from encroaching on this time for meetings or other events.

'Don't touch your box @ night'

This one's a little bit naughty, but I guarantee it will stick! I worked with a team who coined the phrase 'Don't touch your box @ night' to remind them to stay out of their inboxes at night. During your tall break, avoid checking emails (or watching funny YouTube cat videos, or doing a social media check-in or listening to a podcast). In fact, try to make it tech-free time. A study by Rutgers University researchers found that smartphone usage during a break didn't allow the brain to recover from mentally challenging tasks and might result in poorer performance.

Reframe a tall break as a peak-performance tool

If we think of our performance like our fitness, we're more likely to commit to taking breaks.

If you did ten 30-second sprints with a 30-second recovery period between each, your distance for each run/rest period would be very similar (give or take). However, if you tried to sprint solidly for ten minutes without any rest periods, it's unlikely that your speed in the final couple of minutes would match the first couple of minutes. Why? Because you're not giving your muscles and respiratory system time to recover.

Working has similar depleting effects on our brains as physical movement has on our bodies. As knowledge workers, when we work, we use up our brain's glucocorticoids, which are a group of hormones that mediate our stress response. If we don't take regular tall breaks throughout the week, we'll be limping to the finish line. If we take breaks, we give our brains the time they need to recuperate.

Start small

It can sometimes be hard to break up with being busy; taking breaks may not come easily to some people. If you're accustomed to working from the moment you wake up until you fall asleep at night (sometimes on top of your laptop), suddenly having one or two hours of idle time can feel indulgent, if not unnecessary. It can be psychologically jarring.

So, instead of starting with a full hour, block off 15 minutes and see how you feel. Break your old routine by setting an intention – 'Today, I'm just going to rest for 20 minutes by reading a book' – using discipline (acknowledge that you may feel uncomfortable resting) and repetition. Over time, try to increase the time you spend resting. Remember, done is better than perfect, so any time that you can dedicate to resting will help.

Micro-habit 3: Add grande breaks

Some days, a piccolo or tall coffee just won't hit the sides and we need a grande coffee – the largest coffee on the menu. Grande breaks should occur on a weekly basis and ideally be a minimum of one or two full days off, when you disengage completely from work stress and restore your energy. I understand that from time to time you may not be able to take one or two days off in a week – there might be a looming deadline, or you might be working on a complex project. When possible, try to fiercely protect your grande breaks, because perpetually denying yourself the time to switch off is an unhealthy habit that can creep in.

I recently learned through my fabulous fitness coach, Nikki Ellis from Cinch, that weightlifters use 'deload' periods, where they deliberately lower the intensity of their training to enable them to focus on their physical and mental recovery. During deload periods, they typically lift lighter weights or drop the number of sets they do for each exercise. This break allows them to hit their next training cycle with more intensity and, in doing so, lift heavier weights.

This exemplifies the old saying that sometimes you need to slow down to speed up.

We need to reframe our grande breaks in this way too. If we take the time to rest and pause, we'll achieve better results afterwards. For some organisations and leaders, this requires a radical shift in their culture – specifically, away from promoting people who work 'massive hours' and rarely rest, and in doing so subtly rewarding and reinforcing a hustle culture. Again, having clearly articulated norms, practices and principles in the form of digital guardrails can support employees to take breaks.

Here are some ideas for taking grande breaks.

Plan your grande breaks

If you spend some time planning what you might like to do for a grande break, it gives you something to look forward to and creates an anticipatory rise. When you anticipate something that you think will be a positive experience, your brain produces dopamine. So, taking a grande break provides dual benefits: from the anticipation as well as from the actual, tangible experience.

Schedule them in your calendar

We must prioritise the important things in life. These are the things we'll remember on our death beds – not the menial meetings. While we may be tempted to have an exhaustive to-do list with a myriad of tasks we need to perform, what's *really* potent and critical to performing those tasks in an optimal way is rest. It's paramount that we put rest in our calendar. If we fail to schedule our breaks and prioritise rest, and continue to burn the midnight oil, we'll end up burnt out or seriously ill. I can attest to this, as I've experienced burnout on two occasions, when I ignored my body's whispers to rest and kept pushing on. However, if we're proactive about taking regular breaks, there's significantly less risk that we'll walk down the path to burnout.

Plan and protect your weekends

The 'recovery paradox' or 'weekend paradox' suggests that the people who need to recover and rest from their work tend to find that recovery most challenging or elusive. When you have a stressful job, the odds are stacked against you to take time to recover. An analysis of results from 198 separate studies involving employees at work and at home showed that workers with the most mentally and emotionally taxing jobs were the least likely to feel rested and rejuvenated during their time off. In contrast, people with physically demanding jobs, such as farmers and construction workers, had much less trouble winding down.

Research suggests that people who are more stressed at work tend to get less exercise and poorer-quality sleep, which is a recipe for poor health and further perpetuates the stress cycle. To beat the weekend paradox, plan how you want to spend your time off with activities that recharge you. This is highly individual-specific, but research confirms that your recovery time should be dedicated to doing tasks and activities that you want to do, as opposed to what you're obligated to do. Whether you choose to do something that's purely relaxing with no agenda (such as going for a swim in the ocean, or brunch with a friend) or master a new skill (such as painting, stand-up paddleboarding or skateboarding), the main goal is to achieve full psychological detachment from your work.

Plan your holidays

The ultimate grande break is a holiday, during which you have consecutive days (if not weeks) disconnected from your work. However, during the COVID-19 pandemic, many people accrued a lot of annual leave and were reluctant or unable to take holidays. Others have cited the avalanche of emails, Teams messages and additional work upon their return as a reason to defer their holidays. Since the return of domestic and international travel, there's no better time to book a holiday. Again, it's important to put it in your calendar so you remember it and commit to it – just like your other grande breaks, the anticipation of the holiday will also yield positive results.

Wharton School Professor Adam Grant says, 'The holidays shouldn't be a time to recharge. They should be a time to celebrate. If work is exhausting people to the point that they're using their time off to recover, you might have a burnout culture. A healthy organization doesn't leave people drained in the first place.' This is why taking regular piccolo, tall and grande breaks is critical and needs to be a personal responsibility: so many people crawl to the finish line as their annual leave approaches, only to spend the first couple of days of the holidays sick or sleeping.

Summary

1. Take piccolo breaks.
2. Schedule tall breaks.
3. Add grande breaks.

Practice 11

Establish power-down rituals

My mum worked with three young kids, as I do. Growing up, I rarely saw her overwhelmed or frazzled (although she now tells me that was far from reality). In my eyes she was half superwoman and half Olivia Newton-John. She managed to combine a successful career as a teacher, and later as a school leader, with raising three kids.

You know what she didn't have to contend with? Work emails at 7 p.m., 81 WhatsApp messages a day and 10 p.m. Seesaw notifications reminding her that tomorrow is the start of book week. She didn't have to read 27 WhatsApp thumb emoji responses to one message that football training had been cancelled; she simply had to answer one phone call and then call the next person on the list she'd been given at the start of the season. Life was simple. Technology was supposed to make our lives easier and more efficient, but that often doesn't appear to be the case. The productivity paradox supports this claim: the expected productivity gains from digital technologies have not yielded the results we'd hoped for (or been sold), hence why so many of us feel OUSTED.

The boundaries between our personal and professional lives have been obliterated, thanks to mobile devices. After-hours messages and emails mean we rarely feel like we can switch off from our work. The plethora of digital devices (referred to as 'gadget glut' by Alexandra Samuel), coupled with our social media sinkholes, have resulted in many of us existing in a perpetual state of overwhelm. We feel like we have no choice other than to be tethered to technology.

A 2022 study by Cisco reported that, of knowledge workers who had not seen any improvements in their work-life balance since shifting to hybrid work, 70.9 per cent said this was because they couldn't switch off from work. This was consistent across all levels of seniority and all age groups. This is a serious threat to making hybrid work work.

We need to find ways to unplug and switch off from work (and our devices). As more people shift to hybrid or remote work, we can no longer rely on the commute home from the office to signal the end of the workday. We must be more intentional about creating clear finishes to our workdays.

So, what can we do to help us feel like the day is done, especially if we're working from home? Simple: we need to create predictable routines that signal to our brains that the workday is finished.

A solid power-down ritual can help us ease tension that can arise when we don't feel we can shut off because there are unfinished tasks floating around in our heads. If we assign unfinished tasks to another time, we can have some mental respite. A power-down ritual can also kickstart our productivity by providing structure to our following day. If we strategically wrap up our day and put a firm end to it, we can more easily pick up where we left off the next day. It can also force us to pause and examine if we're spending time on the tasks that matter the most.

Let's explore why we need to establish power-down rituals to signal the end of our days. Now that the living room often doubles as the office, it's not always possible to physically leave work, so we have to send clear signals to our brain that our workday is done and enforce tools-down (even with our personal devices). Let's look at three micro-habits to master to help you do this.

Micro-habit 1: Clear cognitive associations

Before the COVID-19 pandemic, most of us had clear lines of demarcation between our work and personal lives. Many of us had a commute to and from the office that signalled the start and end of the day. We had clear physical distinctions between our professional and personal lives. However, the shift to remote or hybrid work has blurred those distinctions. Now, many of us are working and living in the exact same space – if not every day, then for several days per week – and sending our brains mixed signals.

We can help our brains by carving out intentional spaces at home that we reserve, if possible, just for work. If you *don't* have a dedicated workspace, it's hard for your brain to know when to start (or finish) work. Normally, at home, our brains are ready to relax – to spend time with friends or family, eat, sleep and possibly watch Netflix – because that's what we've historically done at home. So, without a dedicated workspace at home, our brains struggle to neurologically transition from work mode to home mode.

Ideally, you'd have a separate workspace – perhaps a small space in your lounge room that can be used as a study nook – but I recognise that this isn't possible for everyone. For me, my dining table doubles as my desk. However, there are simple adjustments you can make to signal where and when you work.

Dr Yousef, in a video series for Headspace, suggests using physical objects such as a tablecloth or scarf to act as visual markers to signal to your brain that you're in a work zone. These physical objects can be removed when your day is done, so your dining table reverts to a place for food and laughter.

Consider what cues you can use to create a congruent cognitive association about when it's time to work and when it's time to rest. Here's how you can create clear cognitive associations.

Have a designated workspace

If you have a specific spot at home for work, such as an office or desk, your brain can more easily transition into and out of work mode. This is probably why the PwC report found that 79 per cent of people who had a dedicated workspace at home reported that their mental health and wellbeing improved when working remotely. The important trick is that when work is over, don't casually sit at your desk or workstation and do non-work activities there, because you'll send the wrong associations to your brain.

Create a hard stop to your workday

It's easy for the workday to keep going and going when you're working at home. You tell yourself you'll finish at 5.30 p.m., and suddenly it's 6.45 p.m. and your partner is calling out to you that dinner is on the table.

Try to plan what 'done' looks like. Can you specify a time, or a number of tasks you need to accomplish? To help you stick to this time, have a post-work activity planned. Meeting a friend for a walk in the local park at 5 p.m. means you're much more likely to stick to your 4.30 p.m. finishing time. Perhaps your workday will end when you've accomplished your three Most Important Tasks (MITs), as Lorraine Murphy suggests.

Close your tabs

Seeing all your tabs open on your computer or laptop, day after day, is like seeing a pseudo to-do list. Closing all your tabs creates a predictable routine to signal it's the end of the day, and it means you'll start the next day with a clean slate and not allow any cognitive residue from previous days to linger. If you have any important tabs that you want to revisit, use a tool like Evernote or OneNote to archive websites.

Create rituals to transition into your evening

Evening transition rituals are patterned behaviours that signal to your brain that the workday is over. Ideally, you'd repeat these activities at the end of every day. Here are some examples of rituals you could try to signal the end of each workday:

- Light a candle or use specific essential oils (this is particularly effective if you have a strong olfactory sense).
- If you have a designated office space, leave it and close the door.
- Put dedicated work items – such as your diary, pens, Post-it notes and laptop – out of sight.
- Listen to a specific playlist that signals that your workday has concluded (remembering to listen to this only at the end of the workday).
- Make a cup of tea.
- Take the dog for a walk.
- Change out of your work clothes (yes, even if you rock the 'wardrobe mullet', where you wear professional attire up top for the Zoom window and have a party happening downstairs with your boardshorts or activewear).

Micro-habit 2: Close down the day

Mentally closing down your day is vital if you want to feel like the workday is done. Many of us have the best intentions to switch off at night, but we have many open mental loops running through our heads. Unfinished tasks or new requests can weigh on our minds, creating stress, anxiety and even productivity guilt:

- *Don't forget to send the email with the PDF to Jess tomorrow.*
- *Remember to reschedule that meeting with the marketing team.*
- *Don't forget that you need to finish that data analysis and send it to the finance team for review.*

If we took the time to properly wrap up our workdays by writing down any loose ends and planning for the day ahead tomorrow, we'd be in a much stronger position to switch off and take some much-needed mental respite. However, few of us take the time either to wrap up the day or prepare for the day ahead. In a world where emails never stop arriving in our inboxes, and there are always another few tasks that we need to add to our ever-growing to-do lists, setting aside some time to close out the day and plan for the next can put us in a psychological state of feeling 'done'.

These are my top tips for closing down your day.

Set aside time to wrap up and plan

Many of us wrap up our days by doing one last swoop of our inboxes, or finishing the eighth Teams meeting of the day and hastily shutting the laptop lid. The problem is that, while we may have physically finished our workday, we haven't done so mentally. Aim to set aside five to ten minutes at the end of each day to wrap up the day and plan for the next day. Set this time in your calendar so you don't forget to do it. Add some prompts to your calendar or paper diary to help scaffold your plan for tomorrow.

Close open loops

Look through today's to-do list to acknowledge what you accomplished. Yes, it's okay to write down all the extra tasks you did and then cross them out if it gives you some satisfaction in doing so!

So often we go from one day to the next without ever really acknowledging our wins. We feel deflated because we don't appear to have made much progress, when the reality is quite different. Take some time to look at what you successfully accomplished today, and celebrate your success. This is particularly important for knowledge workers, who don't often have tangible evidence of their output (unlike a carpenter, for example, who may finish the day and see the frame and gyprock they erected).

Plan for tomorrow

Write your to-do list for tomorrow, following the guidance of Practice 5. Don't write one long laundry list of tasks; otherwise, you can end up with things like 'Reply to Tim's email' next to much more complex tasks like 'Write annual report' that require significantly more time and effort, and this will overload your brain.

Look in your calendar for any meetings or upcoming tasks that need to be prioritised for the next day. Carry over any tasks from today that weren't performed and need to be done tomorrow (or add them to your master to-do list if they won't be actioned tomorrow). Categorise your deep work and shallow work tasks for the next day. Time-block your calendar by allocating your deep work tasks to the time when you're most likely to be alert and focused (remember, this is your chronotype's peak-performance window), and allocate your shallow work tasks outside your mental primetime. Estimate how much time each task will take and put this in your calendar (paper and/or digital) because, remember, work expands to fill the time you give it.

Specify your success

So many of us set vague to-do items. We need to use much more tangible success criteria. So, instead of 'Work on annual report', you could write, 'Draft introductory chapter for the annual report'. It's highly unlikely that you could ever write an entire annual report in one day, so you'd be unable to cross this off your to-do list, which would cause frustration. Completing the introductory chapter in a day is more achievable, so listing this instead gives you the opportunity to accomplish one of your to-do items.

Micro-habit 3: Create digital depots

How many times have you said to yourself, 'I'm going to get an early night tonight'... and, before you know it, 11 p.m. rolls around and you're in bed watching Netflix on your iPad? Or perhaps you promised yourself that your phone is staying out of your bedroom, and somehow you're scrolling social media at 5 a.m. when you woke up early. Yes, it happens to me too.

Mobile technologies mean we can now lie in bed and check Teams messages on our phones. We can be in the kitchen preparing dinner while also dealing with a crisis at work. We can be enjoying dinner with our family and having our phone bark orders at us. Some of us allegedly engage in 'toilet tweeting', where – you guessed it – we use our devices on the toilet!

One of the best things you can do to create firmer lines of demarcation between when you're 'on' and when you're 'off' at home is to create a digital landing zone. This is a designated spot in your house where you put your digital devices when not in use, or when you don't want to be tempted by technology. For example, you might charge your phone in the laundry, or on the dining room sideboard, or in a lockable box in the study.

Having a set spot means that you remove any decision fatigue and save some of your valuable mental resources. Remember, just seeing a device can be a psychological trigger for you to start thinking about it, or it may even nudge you to use it again (when you really don't want to).

Here are some things to consider when setting up landing zones.

Have a phone basket or drawer

I'm sure you've had the experience of walking in the door after a stressful day, greeting your partner with a forced smile to conceal your foul mood and, just when you're convinced your day cannot get any worse, your phone rings and it's your sibling calling with a trivial family matter. Arrgh! Your mood plummets further, and your poor partner is facing your emotional hangover.

What if, instead, you turned your phone to Do Not Disturb before you walked in the door, and then put it in your phone landing zone? Yes, that family matter would still exist, but perhaps your sibling would call you back tomorrow, or send you an SMS, and you could respond at a time when you were in a better head space, instead of being digitally bombarded with more issues.

Having a specific location where phones go in your house can help you (and also your family members) to unplug. This could be a phone basket, a drawer, a timber box or even a lockable box such as those from inchargebox. It really doesn't matter, so long as it's a set spot.

A phone depot is especially great if you have screenagers, because it allows you to create firm digital guardrails about where devices go at set times, such as mealtimes and study hours. It also stops phubbing (phone snubbing). Think of the number of times you've had dinner with your phone on or near the table. When you have family or friends over for dinner, you can encourage them to pop their phones in the basket. It's amazing once you've done this a couple of times how much more engaging and enriching conversations can be.

Author Glennon Doyle shared her phone basket on Instagram, where she has her kids' friends check their phones at the door.

She says, 'They all act exasperated but seem interestingly relieved. Then, after a minute, they look at each other. And talk. And dance and laugh and stuff. And they remember that they are with their friends so there is no need to be anywhere else.' Brené Brown encouraged her children to do the same, reminding them to 'hang up and hang out'.

Studies show that having our phones in our visual proximity can not only distract us but also impair our perceived enjoyment of whatever we're doing. In one experiment, researchers told some restaurant-goers to leave their phones out on the table and others to put them in a box that was out of both reach and sight. At the conclusion of the meal, participants were asked how enjoyable the meal had been and how distracted they felt. Not surprisingly, the people who had their phones on the table felt more distracted, which in turn reduced their enjoyment of the meal, compared to the people whose devices were put in the box.

Research shows that smartphones are also killing our conversations. If there's a phone present when you're in a social interaction, it decreases the quality of what you talk about – you have surface conversations because that's all you can handle when you're distracted – and your empathetic connection decreases because some of your focus is diverted to your phone.

Have a device landing zone

Have a specific spot in your house where your digital devices – such as tablets, laptops or gaming consoles – go at night to charge. If you have screenagers, enforce this with them, too. Two important caveats, though:

1. If they don't whinge and roll their eyes when asked to hand over their device, beware: they may have a decoy device.
2. Be careful that they charge the device and not just the empty case.

Visit the Book Resources page of my website for some handy device storage options.

Summary

1. Clear cognitive associations.
2. Close down the day.
3. Create digital landing zones.

Practice 12

Enjoy mind-wandering mode

I've never had a great idea germinate while I was in my inbox, nor have I ever solved a complex problem while in an Excel spreadsheet. Never. What about you? Where do you do your best thinking? My best ideas, and solutions to problems I've spent months agonising over, come to me in the shower, while I'm running, when I'm on holidays, when I first wake up in the morning or – in the good old days – when I would go on a plane with no wi-fi. Great ideas often come to us when we're 'off', and often when we're bored.

Why is this the case? When we're 'off', our brains enter what neuroscientists call the 'default mode network' (DMN). This is where we daydream. The DMN is a network of brain regions that interact when a person is not focused on the outside world. We turn off our prefrontal cortex, the part of our brain that does our conscious thinking, and enter a mind-wandering mode. It is at this time that we often solve problems or come up with creative ideas.

However, we've lost the art of being bored. It appears that many of us are afflicted with 'solitude deprivation', a term coined by Cal Newport in his book *Digital Minimalism*. We've forgotten what it's like to idle with our thoughts. We now fill every single moment of white space we once had with time on our phones or other devices. The time we once spent daydreaming is now occupied on our phones – the wait at the doctor's surgery, standing at the bus stop, even the brief wait for our morning coffee sees many of us filling the void with mindless scrolling.

Aristotle coined the term 'nature abhors a vacuum', suggesting that the laws of nature and physics demand *every* space be filled with something. I'm convinced this is why my garden is filled with weeds! Today, it's so easy for us to fill the void with a screen.

We've become so accustomed to self-soothing with our screens that we'd rather be electrically shocked than left alone with our thoughts. In a 2016 study, participants were left alone in a lab for 15 minutes. They had the option of self-administering an electric shock to counter their boredom. The results were staggering: even though all participants had previously stated that they would pay money to avoid being shocked with electricity, 67 per cent of males and 25 per cent of females chose to self-administer a small electric shock in lieu of being bored. One data outlier gave themselves 108 shocks during the 15 minutes!

Despite what we've been conditioned to believe, we actually enjoy moments of boredom when we take them, or when they're forced upon us. Research confirms that once people experience being idle with their thoughts, they acknowledge that it's much more pleasurable than they'd anticipated. It's just that many of us have become so used to avoiding this. People enjoy mind-wandering once given the chance to do it, although many admit that they find it strenuous.

Having opportunities, either planned or spontaneous, to allow your mind to wander is vital for your performance in an always-on digital world that's been designed to constantly divert your attention. When your mind drifts here and there, you're more likely to land on solutions to complex problems that you've wrestled with for months, or come up with novel ideas. This is very different to how your brain works when engaging in a cognitively demanding task. Being bored needs to be seen as an incubation period: having time offline when your mind can wander allows you to come up with fresh ideas and new ways to solve problems. As a knowledge worker, mind-wandering time should be a critical component of your working week.

As Brené Brown said, 'It takes courage to say yes to rest and play in a culture where exhaustion is seen as a status symbol'.

Micro-habit 1: Leave white space in your calendar

It sounds ridiculous but, if we don't fiercely protect time to be bored, then chances are it will get crowded out by other activities that we deem to be more 'productive'. You may plan to spend Wednesday afternoon playing nine holes of golf to clear your head, but if it doesn't go in your calendar then, before you know it, a Teams meeting will appear at 4 p.m. and you will need to abandon your solo golf afternoon. You need to 'leave margin for magic', as a friend of mine once said to me.

Here's how you can create more white space in your calendar.

Block out mind-wandering time

We've been conditioned to see mind-wandering as something negative. From a young age, we're often told to get our heads out of the clouds. In a society that emphasises doing and hustle and accomplishment, where focus and determination help us to keep our eye on the prize, freely exploring our thoughts has been frowned upon and seen as frivolous. However, we now know that's not the case.

Many of us still feel uncomfortable with the word 'boredom'. I once worked with an executive who just couldn't bring herself to block out 'boredom' on her calendar, even though she knew it was critical for her role. Instead, she carved out 60 minutes each week for 'mind-wandering time'. Now, this may just be semantics, but she happily put this time in her calendar each week because she knew how important it was for her performance. Another leader I once worked with loved neuroscience, so he used to block his calendar each week with 'activation of the default mode network' time. Do whatever it takes for you to embrace boredom.

Leave margin room in your calendar

Having a completely time-clogged calendar, where every hour of the day is planned with no wriggle room, is a recipe for stress and overwhelm. Things will go wrong: meetings will run over time, your child will have an accident at school and you'll need to pick them up, or your colleague will ask for time-sensitive data analysis. Leave some time in your day for unexpected things to take place. The best thing is that, if you don't end up needing that white space for anything in particular, you now have some time to mind-wander or take a piccolo break.

Follow Google's '20 per cent time' habit

In 2004, Google encouraged their employees to spend 20 per cent of their working week working on or exploring projects that show no promise of paying immediate dividends. It's reported that many of Google's significant advances happened during 20 per cent time, such as Gmail and Google Cardboard.

What can you do to broaden your horizons, develop new skills or look for new opportunities? While 20 per cent of your working week may seem excessive or totally out of reach, can you allocate pockets of time when you can engage in something unrelated to your core role that may advance your thinking? Could you attend a conference or networking event outside your area of expertise? Could you read a book or article outside your niche?

Look for incidental moments

Now that you're aware of how important it is to be bored from time to time, try to capture small, incidental moments to be alone with your thoughts. While waiting at the coffee shop, just stand outside and watch the clouds float by. While waiting for the printer to finish your job, just stand and think. Watching your kids do lap after lap at the swimming pool, sit and daydream (even if it's just for a few minutes). You'll be amazed at what ideas may germinate during this time that you may have once spent scrolling your phone.

To help embed this habit, consider using a phone wallpaper that might nudge you to make better choices around your phone use. Some of my favourites are simple but direct: 'Put your phone down, honey', and, 'You don't need Twitter. Let your mind wander.' My favourite one uses a 4000-week poster to show just how many weeks you have used up; this is based on Oliver Burkeman's book *Four Thousand Weeks*, which is the average number of weeks a human lives for. Some people have found that using a visual trigger, such as an elastic band on their phone, can prompt them to develop healthier phone habits.

Micro-habit 2: Have screen sabbaticals

Now, I want to be very clear at the outset of this micro-habit: I'm not referring to a #digitaldetox where you aim to have a planned and prolonged period *completely* without technology. This isn't about complete digital abstinence. Why? Because, put simply, digital detoxes don't work, and they're unattainable for most of us who don't have the luxury of spending two weeks in a rainforest with no wi-fi.

Despite their growing popularity, there's little scientific evidence that digital detoxes work. Detoxes tend to create a binge-and-purge cycle: we have a weekend offline and then come back on Monday and play catch-up on all the messages and emails we missed. Instead, what's more attainable and sustainable in the long-term is taking screen sabbaticals. These are short periods of time when we try to limit, but not completely restrict, our tech usage. For example, we may try to spend just Sunday mornings screen-free.

Here are my top tips for planning regular screen sabbaticals.

Have a tech sabbath

While you may not be able to have an *entire* day without devices, aiming to have at least some time away from the hustle and bustle of your devices on a regular basis can have a huge impact on your wellbeing.

Emma works at the head office of an airline in Australia. After hearing me speak about the benefits of digitally disconnecting, she started to implement screen-sabbath Sundays for a few hours in the morning. She admits that she was reluctant to do so initially because her phone habits were so entrenched but, after the second week, the tangible benefits of unplugging were such that she continues with this habit two years later. 'I feel a sense of peace knowing that I'm not going to hear a ping or ding and no one is going to bark orders at me – well, at least for four hours. It's a form of psychological respite.'

The summer before writing this book, my family and I went to a farm located in a valley in central New South Wales. Internet and phone coverage was sporadic at best. Now, I admit that the first couple of days were a bit rocky as I became accustomed not to check my phone or reply to emails. However, by about day three, I was feeling so much better just having some time away from the frenetic pace that our digitalised lives impose on us. I instantly noticed how much more relaxed and present I felt, and how much my sleep improved. My nervous system was definitely in a parasympathetic state.

Cut it down, don't cut it out

A study showed that cutting your smartphone use by one hour each day was more effective in improving participants' wellbeing than doing a radical overhaul and going on a strict digital detox. The group that reduced their smartphone usage by just an hour a day was using their phones an average of 30 minutes less each day four months after the study had ended, while the other groups in the study reverted to their old habits. This shows that we don't have to completely give up our phones to feel better. (Phew!) There's possibly an optimal daily usage time, which is referred to as the 'Goldilocks principle': sociologists from Ireland have suggested that there's a sweet spot for adolescents' screen time when it comes to their optimal mental wellbeing, and I believe the same would be true for adults.

Capture moments to your personal hard drive

I remember a time when I was so preoccupied filming my son run in an athletics race that I didn't truly savour the moment. Ironically, I hadn't pressed record on my phone's camera, so I failed to digitally archive the moment as well. I know I'm not alone here: you only need to go to a music concert, school production or New Year's Eve fireworks show to observe a sea of people watching the moment from behind their cameras.

Research tells us that if we take photos on our cameras, our visual recall tends to be very strong, but it is at the expense of our auditory recall, meaning our memory of the whole experience can be compromised. Make a rule to yourself that you'll truly try to absorb a moment when using your phone, rather than just capturing it from behind your camera.

Use tech tools

Research has shown that generic prohibition tools like Screen Time for iOS users and Digital Wellbeing for Android users are effective in minimising people's use of social media networking sites. Are you making use of these generic features on your phone? As I often say, the basics work if you work the basics.

Go for a walk without headphones

Nowadays, if you go for a run, you might listen to a podcast (at 1.5 speed of course). When you cook dinner, you might call your friends. When you hang out the washing, you might listen to an audiobook (also on 1.5 speed).

Walking can help us solve problems and come up with novel ideas. Remember, walking creates optic flow, which calms down our amygdala and reduces our feelings of fear, anxiety and threat. This can put us in a relaxed state and allows ideas to blossom. However, many of us rarely go for a walk without headphones in these days. Can you take some time each week to walk *without* headphones?

Communicate your tech-spectations

If you're going to switch off for a substantial period, ensure that you clearly communicate to key stakeholders how they can reach you if there's an urgent matter. You could use your out-of-office reply or email signature to communicate your digital absence and the appropriate people to contact. Remind people that they can use the 'schedule send' function to re-send the email upon your return. This gives you peace of mind knowing that you can mentally switch off with the assurance that, for all urgent matters, you will be contacted via one medium only. This really helps to tackle the fear of missing out (FOMO) that can often be present when we unplug.

Samantha Unrau, Global Director of Social Media Engagement Ops at Nike, explained on LinkedIn that she took a seven-week sabbatical from work and returned to an empty inbox. How did she achieve this digital utopia that many knowledge workers only dream about? She created an email rule to mark all emails as 'read' and route all emails received in her absence to a folder that she then deleted upon her return to work. She created an out-of-office reply that explained she would not be reading emails during her absence and that all emails would be deleted, and to use the 'send later' feature to re-send the email after the date of her return. More than 10,000 people responded to Samantha's initial post declaring that she'd be deleting emails, and she happily reported that not one person used the 'send later' feature.

Micro-habit 3: Meditate for 12 minutes per day

Now, I'm going to be completely honest with you: when I read research suggesting that between 10 and 12 minutes of daily meditation could change your life, I scoffed. Meditation was something for people who owned yoga mats. As a keen scientist, there's no way I would have considered meditating if it weren't for the body of science behind it. For the six months prior to writing this book, I'd been trying to do a regular (certainly not daily) meditation or guided hypnosis practice. I'm happy to report that I was proven wrong (and that, once again, the science was right): meditation *can* really alter your life. Best of all, you don't need lots of time for it to be effective. (And, no, you don't need to own a yoga mat to do it!) It makes for an ideal piccolo break.

Studies suggest that meditation has substantial cognitive and psychological benefits. Meditation involves sustaining attention on immediate experiences and away from the distractions such as mind-wandering or thinking. When we meditate, there's minimal activity in our DMN. This means we're more adept at being 'in the zone', and fully present and focused on where we are.

The good news is that you don't have to do a 60-minute meditation practice to yield the benefits. Studies have shown that as little as ten minutes of meditation a day (although other research suggests 12 minutes as the minimum effective dose) can yield improvements in attention, focus, creativity, calm, resilience and compassion. Meditation increases the grey-matter density of the hippocampus (the part of the brain critical for learning and memory) and also decreases the grey-matter density of the amygdala (which plays a critical role in managing stress and anxiety).

In her book *Peak Mind*, Dr Amishi Jha shares the science behind why meditation is helpful, particularly for our attention, mental fog and the calmness and clarity many of us crave. Meditation, Jha contends, is like push-ups for your mind. Meditation helps you to be more focused on the task at hand and stops you from being mentally yanked around.

Here are some realistic ways to embed meditation into your day.

Start small

Just as you wouldn't start training for a marathon by running 40 kilometres on your first day, nor should you aim to meditate for 12 minutes (or more) straight up. Take small steps. Start with a couple of minutes each day. Over time, incrementally increase your meditation periods. My experience as an initial sceptic was that, once I had tangible experiences of the benefits, I quickly wanted to spend more time meditating. You may find the same.

Use tech tools

Yes, you read that right. There is a range of websites, YouTube clips, apps (such as Calm, Headspace and Insight Timer) and even digital headbands (I use a Muse EEG-powered headband) that can help you to meditate. You don't have to sign up to a five-day meditation retreat to learn how to meditate (although it would make a great macro-break).

Self-directed hypnosis as an alternative

Science is confirming that self-hypnosis can also yield very positive benefits, especially in terms of managing stress and anxiety. It is an effective therapeutic tool to enter a state of focused attention, a skill that is under threat in our digital world. Dr David Spiegel, regarded as an expert in this domain, has created an eye-roll test to determine your hypnotisability, as around one-third of people cannot be hypnotised. Like meditation, there is a range of self-hypnosis tools and apps available online. I use personalised self-hypnoses from Rachel Crethar and the Reveri app.

Summary

1. Leave white space in your calendar.
2. Have screen sabbaticals.
3. Meditate for 12 minutes per day.

Conclusion

Your human operating system in action

How can you realistically apply some of the micro-habits shared in this book? What does it look like for your human operating system (hOS) to determine how you use technology? How do we operate in a digitally demanding world while also working within our biological constraints? Remember, this book was never about going on a #digitaldetox or aiming for inbox zero; it's all about practical, brain-based strategies we can apply to our digital behaviours so that we can start working with, rather than against, our neurobiology.

So, finally, I thought it would be fun to see how I've walked my talk and applied some of these micro-habits to my workday and life while writing this book (and while also delivering an average of five keynotes a week, doing corporate consultancy work to establish teams' digital guardrails and parenting three young boys). I share this not to be self-indulgent, but rather to reveal what it really looks like to put these micro-habits into practice, and to remind you that they work because the basics work if you work the basics! (I admit that I've also written it because I know we all love to see what happens behind the scenes in people's lives!)

Serendipitously, I agreed to write this book during what turned out to be the busiest period I've ever had in my speaking and consultancy business. This wasn't planned. However, I soon realised that I was on the brink of burnout (yes, for a third time). I was OUSTED, because I'd stopped using the very micro-habits I was writing about in this book. (I promised you at the outset that I wasn't living in any type of digital utopia.) So, I made some adjustments and accommodations, and I can happily say that I'm typing this conclusion in a really good space and I'm certainly not burnt out. Why? I simply started to work in congruence with my brain and body again.

So, here's what a typical day in my life might look like.

Table 13.1: A day in the life of Dr Kristy Goodwin

Time	*Micro-habits*
4–6.30 a.m.	I'm a lion, so I wake up early and write at my kitchen table for an hour before I go to the gym (I always write at the same location when I'm at home for state-dependent recall). I start with a self-hypnosis or a ten-minute meditation. Then I light a candle before I start to work, drink a cup of tea as I work and wear my favourite pink mohair cardigan – these are the congruent cognitive associations that signal it's time to write, and can be easily replicated when I'm in a hotel room. I also turn on as many lights as possible to send a message to my hypothalamus that it's time to be awake. After the gym, I try to walk for 10 to 20 minutes as the sun rises.

Time	*Micro-habits*
6.30–9 a.m.	As a mum to three boys, my mornings are very full. (I try and avoid the word 'busy', even if it's just semantics.) During this time, I take a cold shower (at the end of my lovely, warm shower) for one or two minutes (depending on how brave I feel, and based on the chaos that may or may not be happening outside the bathroom).
9–10.30 a.m.	This is my next work shift. I do a five-minute triage of my inbox. My energy is at its peak now, so I don't want to spend too long in my inbox: I'll do that later in the afternoon when my attention is waning. During this time, my phone is in my timber phone box away from my desk and on 'Focus' mode, where all calls, messages and notifications are silenced apart from those from my husband and my sons' childcare and school. I start my power-up ritual with a cup of tea, a playlist and lighting my candle again (I only ever light this fragrance when I'm working). I do a 90-minute work sprint and then take a piccolo break of between five and ten minutes. Sometimes I go and sit outside in the sun and just close my eyes. Other times I take Tommy, our dog, for a quick walk to the beach. Sometimes, I just walk to our local coffee shop and grab a coffee, and do some long exhalations as I walk there and back. The final ten minutes of my ultradian trough is often spent doing some tasks off my shallow work list, such as making a quick call, replying to an email, reading something or making an appointment.

Time	*Micro-habits*
10.30 a.m.–12.10 p.m.	I do another 90-minute digital dash. This may involve writing, data analysis or any other mentally demanding work because, as a lion, this is still my mental primetime.
12.10–12.40 p.m.	Lunch break. I try and eat outside, weather permitting. I also try and go for another ten-minute walk during this time. This is when I love to leave my headphones at home and just engage in mind-wandering. I'm always amazed at the ideas that germinate during this time (and wish I'd brought my phone so I could capture my ideas).
12.40–1.40 p.m.	Depending on what's required of me and/or my energy levels, I can spend this time delivering a virtual masterclass from my professional home studio or doing some more deep work.
1.40–1.45 p.m.	I will sometimes take another piccolo break so I can power through the afternoon. This is usually just some breathing or non-sleep deep rest.
1.45–3 p.m.	This is my shallow work time, when I do the bulk of my emails and any other administrative work. I might also work on slide decks or schedule social media posts. This is when I try to do any meetings with clients or my team (who all work remotely). I try to batch my meetings, with a buffer break between each one because, remember, our productivity drops by around 22 per cent before any meeting.

Time	*Micro-habits*
1.45–3 p.m. cont.	I tackle some shallow tasks between meetings if there's a longer break time between each one. If I don't have meetings, I read during this time: perhaps a research paper, blog post or article. I'm almost always at an energy slump by 3 p.m.
3–3.30 p.m.	I take a break here, because my eldest two kids are home from school. We have afternoon tea together. I might start some dinner prep or bring in the washing (again, no headphones so I can mind-wander).
3.30–4.30 p.m.	My final shallow work period of the day. This is also when I start my power-down ritual: I triage my to-do list for tomorrow, change out of my work clothes (sometimes I admit I put my dressing gown on, much to my husband and sons' horror), listen to a playlist and make a cup of tea.
4.30–7.30 p.m.	I'm in mum mode, ferrying kids to sport training or unpacking/repacking lunchboxes. I wear blue-light-blocking glasses during this time if I need to jump back on my computer (such as to deliver an evening webinar).
7.30–8.30 p.m.	I try to have a digital curfew around this time (try), as I like to be asleep around 8.30 p.m. I know, I know, that's ridiculously early, but I'm hopeless after 9 p.m. I often read fiction before bed and have a warm shower so it's easier to fall asleep. If I do happen to sneak onto my phone at night, I always try to wear my blue-light-blocking glasses.

After reading this book, I'm guessing you're feeling one of two ways: pumped and ready to go, or overwhelmed by all the micro-habits and adjustments you want to make. (With 36 micro-habits in this book, I know it's easy to experience infobesity.) Either way, I encourage you to just make a start. Make small incremental shifts. Don't try to eat the whole watermelon in one mouthful and try to radically overhaul all your digital habits. Instead, just take small bites. Implement one (or possibly two) micro-habits at a time, and then stack more micro-habits on top of these over time.

Air navigation experts use a rule of thumb called the '1 in 60 rule'. It suggests that for every 1 degree a plane veers off its course, it misses it's planned destination by 1 mile for every 60 miles that you fly. What I think this rule also shows is that even small adjustments (1-degree turns are miniscule) can yield big differences further down the track. The same is true with your digital habits: making small, seemingly insignificant changes can have huge implications over time.

My suggestion is to start with a micro-habit that will have a ripple effect. Go back to each practice and select a few that you want to implement. I don't suggest that you make radical shifts and plan a complete digital overhaul. Start small. Implement one or two micro-habits at a time, and once they become embedded, pick a couple more to try.

What lever can you pull that will have most impact? Remember, as humans we have some basic biological constraints that we simply cannot outperform. Our most basic needs are that we sleep, move, connect, breathe, eat and have sunlight exposure. Which of your tech habits would have the greatest impact on these basic needs?

For some of you, it's rectifying sleep. For others it may be increasing your physical movement throughout your day, or bundling your notifications. Perhaps you're going to start by implementing a digital curfew, or putting your phone away in another room while you're working. Over time, those micro-habits can have a substantial impact on your wellbeing and performance.

I recently met a palliative care nurse who's been caring for people in the final days of their lives for over 30 years. She's found that people have common life regrets consistent with those detailed in the book *The Top Five Regrets of the Dying* by Bronnie Ware. However, she's noticed a sixth regret in recent years, particularly among younger people who are in their final stage of life: they wish they'd spent less time on their phones and laptops! These devices have been engineered to rob us of our two most important resources as humans: our time and attention.

Yes, it's hard to resist the digital pull that lures many of us into the digital vortex. However, you have a choice: continue with the toxic tech habits you had before reading the book, or implement some of the micro-habits I've shared and tame your digital behaviours. I don't want you to reflect on your life and wish you'd spent less time tethered to technology.

Start to use your digital devices by design, not by default. Now is your time to thrive in the digital world.

Connect with me

Want to access the resources mentioned throughout this book? Go to:

www.drkristygoodwin.com/deardigital

Want to get your dopamine hit on social media? Then connect online (the irony isn't lost on me):

Website: drkristygoodwin.com

LinkedIn: linkedin.com/in/dr-kristy-goodwin

Instagram: instagram.com/drkristy

Acknowledgements

The ideas in this book would have certainly been reserved for my clients' keynotes and remained ruminating in my head, or shared in random social media posts, had it not been for the encouragement of family, friends and colleagues: 'You need to write another book.'

While I smiled and nodded at their suggestion, I genuinely didn't think that I had the time to write another book. As this wasn't my first rodeo, I knew the time involved and I was time poor. Really time poor.

As a mum to three boys, with a very full speaking schedule, I convinced myself that I didn't have the bandwidth to write a book.

Then I thought, *what if I could use this busy period to write my book?* This would force me to test the micro-habits that I planned to write about if I ever wrote a book again. If I could write a book during an intense period in my business, surely that would provide a proof of concept for the strategies I was writing about. And so, I took the challenge.

As an academic, I find writing cathartic. It's a bit like therapy. Writing this book has forced me to organise my ideas coherently and synthesise the years of research I've consumed.

Now, don't be duped into thinking this has been an easy process: it hasn't. I haven't been tucked away writing this book during a writer's retreat while sipping cappuccinos. This book has been written in airport lounges, hotel rooms and at my dining table, in between keynotes and mum life (many a paragraph was written in the car while I waited to collect my sons from school). I've really had to apply the micro-habits in this book to ensure I had enough focused time to write and that my stress was managed. I had to prioritise the potent things in my life while I brought this book to life, which meant saying no to a lot of things.

Truth be told, about three-quarters of the way through, I stopped applying some of the micro-habits I was writing about. The wheels fell off. I was on the brink of burnout *again*. I started to multi-task, I wasn't switching my devices off before sleep, I was working for long stretches without taking regular breaks, and I wasn't taking the time to digitally disconnect. I'd abandoned my to-do list (because I was convinced *everything* was urgent and important), I'd started writing with my phone next to my laptop and I was nibbling on my inbox. I was too tired to work with my chronotype. I was a mess.

After some tough conversations with mentors and friends, I was forced to confront the harsh reality that I needed to practice what I preach. So, I started to apply the micro-habits that I knew would serve me, that help me to thrive in the digital world – the micro-habits I share in this book. And I'm pleased to report that I turned the ship around. Despite having a *very* full calendar and a stringent writing routine, I flourished. I managed to bypass burnout.

It would be remiss of me not to acknowledge the sacrifices that were made by many people to help bring this book to life, and especially to those who helped me course-correct when I was veering off.

To Nick, my patient and supportive husband, who endured his (un)fair share of my techno-tantrums and tears as I wrote this book. Your tear-wiping, encouragement and unrelenting support have been my bedrock. For all the extra hours I've had to disappear so I could write without interruption, your understanding hasn't gone unnoticed. Thank you for everything.

To my three gorgeous boys, Taj, Billy and Ashton: thanks for asking about my book, for helping me pick a cover design and for all the extra days and nights you've had as 'boys' nights' while I've been away for work or hiding somewhere so you couldn't distract me. Your afternoons of extra screen time are coming to an abrupt end now that I'm not bogged down writing this book!

Billy, you are the reason I wrote this book: it was the awful accident that you had climbing on the lounge, falling off and smashing your face when I was digitally distracted, that nudged me to acknowledge that I had toxic tech habits. Even as someone who researches and writes about this topic, I'm not immune to the digital pull. Your little scar on your lip is a daily reminder to me of why this work is so important. If we don't control technology, it will control us (as it did me on that fateful day in 2015).

Thank you to my family, who supported me while I wrote this book. Thanks especially to my parents and parents-in-law for *all* the extra baby-sitting, meals and help you've offered our family over the years, especially during the months I got swallowed up by this manuscript. It's greatly appreciated. Mum, thanks as always for inspiring me and reminding me of what's important.

To friends and neighbours who have asked me about my book progress and sent messages, memes and meals to keep me going: thank you for your sustenance.

To clients who have genuinely invested in their teams' digital wellbeing and performance with keynotes, masterclasses, digital guardrail consultancy work, offsites and digital wellbeing products: thanks for your ongoing support. A special thanks to clients who did the digital pirouette with me during the pandemic, as I shifted from on-stage speaking to online speaking (and for forgiving me when I turned up to Zoom calls as 'Stinky Bum-Bum' when my son decided to change my name on Zoom when he used my Zoom account for home-schooling, or for the time I delivered a virtual keynote as a unicorn avatar that I couldn't disable after they'd used Snap Camera).

To team K:

- To Kathy Rhodes from the Thought Alchemists, who's helped my business to thrive: thanks for indulging in my love of all things alliteration, for responding to my (many) WhatsApp messages of despair and, most of all, for inspiring me to be the best version of myself.
- To Karen: thank you for your unwavering support of my business. Your dotting of the i's and crossing of the t's and sorting out all my digital dilemmas with grace and speed is greatly appreciated. Thanks for protecting 'future Kristy', for managing my calendar like a ninja, and for helping me see things in my business I simply cannot.
- To Kathleen: thank you for all the things you do to make my business run. Your support over the years has been invaluable.
- To Kelly Irving: thank you for the countless hours spent helping me synthesise my ideas and gently reminding me that I didn't want to add to the readers' infobesity. It's been a joy to work with you. Can't wait to do it again. Yes, I have already mapped out the next book!

Thank you to the fabulous team at Major Street Publishing, who have helped me to birth this book.

- To Lesley: thank you for the opportunity to publish my book in record speed, and for your constant encouragement.
- To Will: thanks for your fastidious attention to detail and for helping me to strengthen my manuscript.
- To Eleanor: thank you for your strategic thinking and marketing prowess, which has enabled this book to get into so many hands.

Finally, thanks to you, the reader, who's bravely tackled a topic that I know is confronting and that you would probably prefer to avoid. Thanks for your willingness to tame your digital behaviours. It's time for more of us to thrive in the distracted world.

Sources

Preface: Warning – your digital diagnosis

Eyesafe, 'COVID-19: screen time spikes to over 13 hours per day according to Eyesafe Nielsen estimates', 28 March 2020, eyesafe.com/covid-19-screen-time-spike-to-over-13-hours-per-day/.

G Dixon, 'Aussies spend almost 17 years in a lifetime staring at their phones', *Reviews.org*, 7 April 2021, reviews.org/au/mobile/aussie-screentime-in-a-lifetime/.

J Taylor, '40% of young adults admitted to using Twitter on the toilet, rest are lying', *Yahoo News*, 13 February 2014, news.yahoo.com/40-young-adults-admitted-using-twitter-toilet-rest-141931025.html.

Yellow Social Media Report 2020, accessed 21 October 2022, yellow.com.au/wp-content/uploads/sites/2/2020/07/Yellow-Social-Media-Report-2020-Consumer-Statistics.pdf.

J Spataro, '2 years of digital transformation in 2 months', Microsoft blog, 30 April 2020, microsoft.com/en-us/microsoft-365/blog/2020/04/30/2-years-digital-transformation-2-months/.

Microsoft, 'Research proves your brain needs breaks: new options help you carve out downtime between meetings', 20 April 2021, microsoft.com/en-us/worklab/work-trend-index/brain-research.

Microsoft, *2021 Work Trend Index: Annual Report*, 22 March 2021, ms-worklab.azureedge.net/files/reports/hybridWork/pdf/2021_Microsoft_WTI_Report_March.pdf.

J Yun, '"Create disruptions": Why Atlassian's Dom Price has no work routine', *Yahoo Finance*, 19 October 2020, au.finance.yahoo.com/news/atlassian-dom-price-202624713.html

Introduction: Overload – digital burnout!

DJ Levitin, 'Why it's so hard to pay attention, explained by science', *Fast Company*, 23 September 2015, fastcompany.com/3051417/why-its-so-hard-to-pay-attention-explained-by-science.

id, *The organized mind: Thinking straight in the age of information overload*, Dutton, New York, 2014.

RE Bohn, (2009). *How much information? 2009 Report on American Consumers*, University of California, San Diego, 2009.

RE Bohn & J Short, 'Measuring consumer information', *International Journal of Communication*, vol. 6, no. 1, 2012, pp. 980–1000.

S Heim & A Keil, 'Too much information, too little time: how the brain separates important from unimportant things in our fast-paced media world', *Frontiers for Young Minds*, 1 June 2017, kids.frontiersin.org/articles/10.3389/frym.2017.00023.

J Zverina, 'U.S. media consumption to rise to 15.5 hours a day – per person – by 2015', *UC San Diego Today*, 6 November 2013, today.ucsd.edu/story/u.s._media_consumption_to_rise_to_15.5_hours_a_day_per_person_by_2015.

ER Kandel, JH Schwartz, TM Jessell, et al (eds), *Principles of Neural Science*, vol. 4, McGraw Hill, New York, 2000, pp. 1227–1246.

L Weaver, *The Invisible Load: A Guide to Overcoming Stress & Overwhelm*, Little Green Frog Publishing, 2019.

EL Deci & MR Ryan, 'Self-determination theory', in PAM Van Lange, AW Kruglanski & ET Higgins (eds), *Handbook of Theories of Social Psychology*, vol. 1, Sage, Thousand Oaks, CA, 2012, pp. 416–437.

The Social Dilemma, motion picture, 2020.

T Haynes, 'Dopamine, smartphones & you: a battle for your time', *Science in the News*, 1 May 2018, sitn.hms.harvard.edu/flash/2018/dopamine-smartphones-battle-time/.

A Cooper, 'What is "brain hacking"? Tech insiders on why you should care', *CBS News*, 9 April 2017, cbsnews.com/news/brain-hacking-tech-insiders-60-minutes/.

M Honma, Y Masaoka, N Iizuka, et al, 'Reading on a smartphone affects sigh generation, brain activity, and comprehension'. *Scientific Reports*, vol. 12, 2022, pp. 1–8.

American Psychological Association, *Stress in America 2021: Stress and Decision-making During the Pandemic*, 2021, apa.org/news/press/releases/stress/2021/decision-making-october-2021.pdf.

J Norquay 'How Many Emails Are Sent Per Day In 2022?', Prosperity Media blog, 16 April 2021, prosperitymedia.com.au/how-many-emails-are-sent-per-day-in-2022/.

Microsoft, *2022 Work Trend Index: Annual Report*, 16 March 2022, microsoft.com/en-us/worklab/work-trend-index/great-expectations-making-hybrid-work-work.

E Nagoski & A Nagoski, *Burnout: The Secret to Unlocking the Stress Cycle*, Ballantine Books, 2019.

A May, interview with author, 2022.

L Murphy, *Step Into You: How to Rediscover Your Extraordinary Self*, Hachette, 2021.

L Corduff, 'The survey on women: sleep, stress, sex and more', unpublished survey, data collected October 2022.

J Chan & S Clarke, *2021 Global Workplace Burnout Study*, Infinite Potential, infinite-potential.com.au/2021-global-burnout-study.

Microsoft, *Work Trend Index: Hybrid Work Is Just Work. Are We Doing It Wrong?* 22 September 2022, assets.ctfassets.net/y8fb0rhks3b3/1vMxzsKg3F41x6RwBXxgOj/101137360f99abf0a268905bdc63f9e9/2022_Work_Trend_Index_Pulse_Report_Sep-3697-.pdf/

A Bayes, G Tavella & G Parker, 'The biology of burnout: causes and consequences', *The World Journal of Biological Psychiatry*, vol. 22, no. 9, 2021, pp. 686–698.

T Kakiashvili, J Leszek & K Rutkowski, 'The medical perspective on burnout', *International Journal of Occupational Medicine and Environmental Health*, vol. 26, no. 3, 2013, pp. 401–412.

World Health Organization, 'Burn-out an "occupational phenomenon": International Classification of Diseases', 28 May 2019, who.int/news/item/28-05-2019-burn-out-an-occupational-phenomenon-international-classification-of-diseases.

L Weaver, op. cit.

C Groeschel, *Winning the War in Your Mind: Change Your Thinking, Change Your Life*, Zondervan, 2021.

EFM Wijdicks, 'The ascending reticular activating system', *Neurocritical Care*, vol. 31, no. 2, 2019, pp. 419–422.

A Fraser, *The Third Space: Using Life's Little Transitions to Find Balance and Happiness*, Random House, 2012.

A Fraser, 'The perfect storm of burnout', Dr Adam Fraser blog, 16 November 2021, dradamfraser.com/blog-content/2021/11/16/rechargeable.

The E-Lab & Deakin University, *The Wellbeing of Financial Advisers in Australia Report*, 2021, dradamfraser.com/e-lab/financial-advisers-report.

VA Petruo, M Mückschel & C Beste, 'On the role of the prefrontal cortex in fatigue effects on cognitive flexibility – a system neurophysiological approach', *Scientific Reports*, vol. 8, no. 1, 2018, pp. 1–13.

Microsoft, 'Research proves your brain needs breaks: new options help you carve out downtime between meetings', 20 April 2021, microsoft.com/en-us/worklab/work-trend-index/brain-research.

ET Hall, 'A system for the notation of proxemic behavior', *American Anthropologist*, vol. 65, no. 5, 2009, pp. 1003–1026.

DJ Levitin. *The organized mind: Thinking straight in the age of information overload*, Dutton, New York, 2014.

E Hatfield, JT Cacioppo & RL Rapson, 'Emotional contagion', *Current Directions in Psychological Science*, vol. 2, no. 3, 1993, pp. 96–100.

SG Barsade, 'The ripple effect: emotional contagion and its influence on group behavior', *Administrative Science Quarterly*, vol. 47, no. 4, 2002, pp. 644–675.

AD Kramer, JE Guillory & JT Hancock, 'Experimental evidence of massive-scale emotional contagion through social networks', *Proceedings of the National Academy of Sciences of the United States of America*, vol. 111, no. 24, 2014, pp. 8788–8790.

K Aubusson, 'The "frightening" effects of the phone messages waking us at night', *The Sydney Morning Herald*, 17 October 2019, smh.com.au/national/the-frightening-effects-of-the-phone-messages-waking-us-at-night-20191016-p5314z.html.

T-W Lin & Y-M Kuo, 'Exercise benefits brain function: the monoamine connection', *Brain Sciences*, vol. 3, no. 1, 2013, pp. 39–53.

B Noudoost & T Moore, 'The role of neuromodulators in selective attention', *Trends in Cognitive Sciences*, vol. 15, no. 12, 2011, pp. 585–591.

Huberman Lab, 'Optimizing Workspace for Productivity, Focus, & Creativity', podcast, 31 January 2022, hubermanlab.com/optimizing-workspace-for-productivity-focus-and-creativity/.

id, 'The Science of Vision, Eye Health & Seeing Better', podcast, 14 June 2021, hubermanlab.com/the-science-of-vision-eye-health-and-seeing-better/.

C Blume, C Garbazza & M Spitschan, 'Effects of light on human circadian rhythms, sleep and mood', *Somnologie*, vol. 23, no. 3, 2019, pp. 147–156.

The National Institute for Occupational Safety and Health (NIOSH), 'Effects of light', Centers for Disease Control and Prevention, reviewed 1 April 2020, cdc.gov/niosh/emres/longhourstraining/light.html.

Huberman Lab, 'Using Light (Sunlight, Blue Light & Red Light) to Optimize Health', podcast, 18 April 2022, hubermanlab.com/using-light-sunlight-blue-light-and-red-light-to-optimize-health/.

LS Eppenberger & V Sturm, 'The role of time exposed to outdoor light for myopia prevalence and progression: a literature review', *Clinical Ophthalmology*, vol. 14, 2020, pp. 1875–1890.

SA Read, MJ Collins & SJ Vincent, 'Light exposure and eye growth in childhood', *Investigative Ophthalmology & Visual Science*, vol. 56, no. 11, 2015, pp. 6779–6787.

L Stone, 'Just breathe: building the case for email apnea', *Huffpost*, 8 February 2008, huffpost.com/entry/just-breathe-building-the_b_85651.

B Robinson, 'Is your computer screen stealing your breath? 6 tips to avoid risks of screen apnea', *Forbes*, 14 November 2020, forbes.com/sites/bryanrobinson/2020/11/14/is-your-computer-screen-stealing-your-breath-6-tips-to-avoid-screen-apnea/.

Mercenary Trader, 'Screen apnea', *Insider*, 31 July 2013, businessinsider.com/screen-apnea-2013-9.

P Taylor, *Death by Comfort: How modern life is killing us and what we can do about it*, Major Street Publishing, Melbourne, 2022.

K McGonigal, *The Upside of Stress: Why Stress Is Good for You, and How to Get Good at It*, Avery, 2016.

Practice 1: Set your digital guardrails

Microsoft, 'The rise of the triple peak day', accessed 20 October 2022, microsoft.com/en-us/worklab/triple-peak-day.

A Zadow, 'Do you answer emails outside work hours? Do you send them? New research shows how dangerous this can be', *The Mandarin*, 14 July 2021, themandarin.com.au/162994-do-you-answer-emails-outside-work-hours-do-you-send-them-new-research-shows-how-dangerous-this-can-be.

Philips, 'Philips survey reveals COVID-19's negative impact on sleep quality and CPAP use', 10 March 2021, philips.com/a-w/about/news/archive/standard/news/press/2021/20210310-philips-survey-reveals-covid-19-s-negative-impact-on-sleep-quality-and-cpap-use.html.

Eyesafe, op. cit.

A Wiehler, F Branzoli, I Adanyeguh, et al, 'A neuro-metabolic account of why daylong cognitive work alters the control of economic decisions', *Current Biology*, vol. 32, no. 16, 2022, pp. 3564–3575.

VA Petruo, M Mückschel & C Beste, op. cit.

A-M Chang, D Aeschbach, JF Duffy & CA Czeisler, 'Evening use of light-emitting eReaders negatively affects sleep, circadian timing, and next-morning alertness', *Proceedings of the National Academy of Sciences of the United States of America*, vol. 112, no. 4, 2015, pp. 1232–1237.

M Walker, *Why We Sleep: Unlocking the Power of Sleep and Dreams*, Scribner, 2017.

Harvard Health Publishing, 'Understanding the stress response: chronic activation of this survival mechanism impairs health', 6 July 2020, health.harvard.edu/staying-healthy/understanding-the-stress-response.

Queensland Brain Institute, 'The limbic system', accessed 20 October 2022, qbi.uq.edu.au/brain/brain-anatomy/limbic-system.

K Aubusson, op. cit.

TL Overton, TE Rives, C Hecht, et al, 'Distracted driving: prevalence, problems, and prevention', *International Journal of Injury Control and Safety Promotion*, vol. 22, no. 3, 2015, pp. 187–192.

M Leekha, M Goswami, RR Shah, et al, 'Are you paying attention? Detecting distracted driving in real-time', *2019 IEEE Fifth International Conference on Multimedia Big Data (BigMM)*, 2019, pp. 171–180.

MR Flaherty, AM Kim, MD Salt & LK Lee, 'Distracted driving laws and motor vehicle crash fatalities', *Pediatrics*, vol. 145, no. 6, 2020, e20193621.

K Garner-Hamilton, interview with author, 2022.

J Clear, *Atomic Habits: Tiny changes, remarkable results: an easy & proven way to build good habits & break bad ones*, Avery, New York, 2018.

JN Bailenson, 'Nonverbal overload: a theoretical argument for the causes of Zoom fatigue', *Technology, Mind, and Behavior*, vol. 2, no. 1, 2021.

E. Peper, V Wilson, M Martin & E Rosegard, 'Avoid Zoom fatigue, be present and learn', *NeuroRegulation*, vol. 8, no. 1, 2021, pp. 47–56.

H Nesher Shoshan & W Wehrt, 'Understanding "Zoom fatigue": a mixed-method approach', *Applied Psychology: An International Review*, vol. 71, no. 3, 2022, pp. 827–852.

S Toney, J Light & A Urbaczewski, A, 'Fighting Zoom fatigue: keeping the zoombies at bay', *Communications of the Association for Information Systems*, vol. 48, 2021.

Practice 2: Boost your focus and reduce technostress

G Markowsky, 'Information theory', *Encyclopedia Britannica*, 9 August 2022, britannica.com/science/information-theory/Physiology.

Short Wave, 'Understanding Unconscious Bias', podcast, 15 July 2020, npr.org/2020/07/14/891140598/understanding-unconscious-bias.

D DiSalvo, 'Your brain sees even when you don't', *Forbes*, 22 June 2013, forbes.com/sites/daviddisalvo/2013/06/22/your-brain-sees-even-when-you-dont/.

S Yousef, *The Science of Productivity and Performance in Our Busy, Always-on World*, accessed 20 October 2022, hr.berkeley.edu/sites/default/files/science_of_wfh_productivity_and_well-being_-_now_conference.pdf.

id, 'Overcoming burnout in a distributed world', Asana blog, 13 April 2021, blog.asana.com/2021/04/dr-yousef-burnout/.

Berkeley Haas Alumni Network, 'The Science of Energy Management and Focus', video, YouTube, 29 January 2021, youtube.com/watch?v=nlNJjeF-Tp8.

L Stone, op. cit.

M Razali Salleh, 'Life event, stress and illness', *The Malaysian Journal of Medical Sciences*, vol. 15, no. 4, 2008, pp. 9–18.

Y-Z Liu, Y-X Wang & C-L Jiang, 'Inflammation: the common pathway of stress-related diseases', *Frontiers in Human Neuroscience*, vol. 11, 2017, p. 316.

K Dhama, SK Latheef, M Dadar, et al, 'Biomarkers in stress related diseases/disorders: diagnostic, prognostic, and therapeutic values', *Frontiers in Molecular Biosciences*, vol. 6, 2019, p. 91.

LS Vidotto, CR Fernandes de Carvalho, A Harvey & M Jones, 'Dysfunctional breathing: what do we know?', *Jornal Brasileiro de Pneumologia*, vol. 45, no. 1, 2019, e20170347.

American Psychological Association, 'Stress effects on the body', 1 November 2018, www.apa.org/topics/stress/body.

H Selye, 'The nature of stress', *Basal Facts*, vol. 7, no. 1, 1985, pp. 3–11.

KE Lee, KJH Williams, LD Sargent, et al, '40-second green roof views sustain attention: the role of micro-breaks in attention restoration', *Journal of Environmental Psychology*, vol. 42, 2015, pp. 182–189.

LS Franco, DF Shanahan & RA Fuller, 'A review of the benefits of nature experiences: more than meets the eye', *International Journal of Environmental Research and Public Health*, vol. 14, no. 8, 2017, p. 864.

SC Van Hedger, HC Nusbaum, L Clohisy, et al, 'Of cricket chirps and car horns: The effect of nature sounds on cognitive performance', *Psychonomic Bulletin & Review*, vol. 26, no. 2, 2019, pp. 522–530.

GN Bratman, GC Daily, BJ Levy & JJ Gross, 'The benefits of nature experience: improved affect and cognition', *Landscape and Urban Planning*, vol. 138, 2015, pp. 41–50.

SR Kellert & EO Wilson, *The Biophilia Hypothesis*, Island Press, Washington, DC, 1993.

Y Joye & A de Block, '"Nature and I are two": a critical examination of the biophilia hypothesis', *Environmental Values*, vol. 20, no. 2, 2011, pp. 189–215.

E Gullone, 'The biophilia hypothesis and life in the 21st century: increasing mental health or increasing pathology?', *Journal of Happiness Studies*, vol. 1, no. 3, 2000, pp. 293–322.

B Jiang, C-Y Chang & WC Sullivan, 'A dose of nature: tree cover, stress reduction, and gender differences', *Landscape and Urban Planning*, vol. 132, 2014, pp. 26–36.

EY Choe, A Jorgensen & D Sheffield, 'Does a natural environment enhance the effectiveness of Mindfulness-Based Stress Reduction (MBSR)? Examining the mental health and wellbeing, and nature connectedness benefits', *Landscape and Urban Planning*, vol. 202, 2020, 103886.

W Yao, X Zhang & Q Gong, 'The effect of exposure to the natural environment on stress reduction: A meta-analysis', *Urban Forestry & Urban Greening*, vol. 57, 2021, 126932.

H Ohly, MP White, BW Wheeler, et al, 'Attention Restoration Theory: A systematic review of the attention restoration potential of exposure to natural environments', *Journal of Toxicology and Environmental Health. Part B, Critical Reviews*, vol. 19, no. 7, 2016, pp. 305–343.

C Crossan & A Salmoni, 'A simulated walk in nature: testing predictions from the Attention Restoration Theory', *Environment and Behavior*, vol. 53, no. 3, 2021, pp. 277–295.

MR Hunter, BW Gillespie & SY-P Chen, 'Urban nature experiences reduce stress in the context of daily life based on salivary biomarkers', *Frontiers in Psychology*, vol. 10, 2019, p. 722.

Huberman Lab, 'Using Light (Sunlight, Blue Light & Red Light) to Optimize Health', podcast, 18 April 2022, hubermanlab.com/using-light-sunlight-blue-light-and-red-light-to-optimize-health/.

YF Li, L Dong & WB Wei, 'Research progress in relationship between vitamin D and myopia and its mechanisms', *Zhonghua Yan Ke Za Zhi (Chinese Journal of Ophthalmology)*, vol. 57, no. 6, 2021, pp. 470–476.

CM McKnight, JC Sherwin, S Yazar, et al, 'Myopia in young adults is inversely related to an objective marker of ocular sun exposure: the Western Australian Raine cohort study', *American Journal of Ophthalmology*, vol. 158, no. 5, 2014, pp. 1079–1085.

S Yazar, AW Hewitt, LJ Black, et al, 'Myopia is associated with lower vitamin D status in young adults' *Investigative Ophthalmology & Visual Science*, vol. 55, no. 7, 2014, pp. 4552–4559.

A Radwan, L Barnes, R DeResh, et al, 'Effects of active microbreaks on the physical and mental well-being of office workers: a systematic review', *Cogent Engineering*, vol. 9, no. 1, 2022, 2026206.

E Watts, '10-minute "micro-breaks" may help prevent worker burnout, study finds', *Medical News Today*, 31 August 2022, medicalnewstoday.com/articles/10-minute-micro-breaks-may-help-prevent-worker-burnout-study-finds.

P Albulescu, I Macsinga, A Rusu, et al, '"Give me a break!" a systematic review and meta-analysis on the efficacy of micro-breaks for increasing well-being and performance', *PLoS One*, vol. 17, no. 8, 2022, e0272460.

C Chen, Y Mochizuki, K Hagiwara, et al, 'Regular vigorous-intensity physical activity and walking are associated with divergent but not convergent thinking in Japanese young adults', *Brain Sciences*, vol. 11, no. 8, 2021, p. 1046.

LD de Voogd, JW Kanen, DA Neville, et al, 'Eye-movement intervention enhances extinction via amygdala deactivation', *The Journal of Neuroscience*, vol. 38, no. 40, 2018, pp. 8694–8706.

E Vlemincx, I Van Diest & O Van den Bergh, 'A sigh of relief or a sigh to relieve: the psychological and physiological relief effect of deep breaths', *Physiology & Behavior*, vol. 165, 2016, pp. 127–135.

LJ Severs, E Vlemincx & J-M Ramirez, 'The psychophysiology of the sigh: I: the sigh from the physiological perspective', *Biological Psychology*, vol. 170, 2022, 108313.

MC Melnychuk, PM Dockree, RG O'Connell, et al, 'Coupling of respiration and attention via the locus coeruleus: effects of meditation and pranayama', *Psychophysiology*, vol. 55, no. 9, 2018, e13091.

S Scott, interview with author, 2022.

Asurion, 'Americans check their phones 96 times a day', *PR Newswire*, 21 November 2019, prnewswire.com/news-releases/americans-check-their-phones-96-times-a-day-300962643.html.

Practice 3: Optimise your workspace

A Goolsbee, 'The battles to come over the benefits of working from home', *The New York Times*, 20 July 2021, nytimes.com/2021/07/20/business/remote-work-pay-bonus.html.

The Productivity Commission, *Working from home: Research paper*, September 2021, pc.gov.au/research/completed/working-from-home/working-from-home.pdf.

R Browne, '70% of people globally work remotely at least once a week, study says', *CBNC*, 30 May 2018, cnbc.com/2018/05/30/70-percent-of-people-globally-work-remotely-at-least-once-a-week-iwg-study.html.

PwC, *PwC's US Remote Work Survey*, 12 January 2021, pwc.com/us/en/services/consulting/business-transformation/library/covid-19-us-remote-work-survey.html.

id, *Balancing Act: The New Equation in hybrid working*, 2022, pwc.com.au/futureofwork.

B Sarkar, 'Six in 10 employees sit for almost nine hours at work: survey' *The Economic Times*, 22 February 2022, economictimes.indiatimes.com/jobs/six-in-10-employees-sit-for-almost-nine-hours-at-work-survey/articleshow/89742664.cms.

Open Access Government, 'Office works spend 75% of their waking hours sitting down', 14 August 2019, openaccessgovernment.org/office-workers-sitting-down/71612/.

CN Waters, EP Ling, AHY Chu, et al, 'Assessing and understanding sedentary behaviour in office-based working adults: a mixed-method approach', *BMC Public Health*, vol. 16, 2016, p. 360.

Better Health Channel, 'The dangers of sitting: why sitting is the new smoking', accessed 21 October 2022, betterhealth.vic.gov.au/health/healthyliving/the-dangers-of-sitting.

M Giurgiu, R Nissen, G Müller, et al, 'Drivers of productivity: being physically active increases yet sedentary bouts and lack of sleep decrease work ability' *Scandinavian Journal of Medicine & Science in Sports*, vol. 31, no. 10, 2021, pp. 1921-1931.

T Koyama, N Kuriyama, E Ozaki, et al, 'Sedentary time is associated with cardiometabolic diseases in a large Japanese population: a cross-sectional study', *Journal of Atherosclerosis and Thrombosis*, vol. 27, no. 10, 2020, pp. 1097–1107.

JH Park, JH Moon, HJ Kim, et al, 'Sedentary lifestyle: overview of updated evidence of potential health risks', *Korean Journal of Family Medicine*, vol. 41, no. 6, 2020, pp. 365–373.

American Heart Association, 'American Heart Association recommendations for physical activity in adults and kids', accessed 21 October 2022, heart.org/en/healthy-living/fitness/fitness-basics/aha-recs-for-physical-activity-in-adults.

Huberman Lab, 'Maximizing Productivity, Physical & Mental Health with Daily Tools', podcast, 12 July 2021, hubermanlab.com/maximizing-productivity-physical-and-mental-health-with-daily-tools/.

id, 'Optimizing Workspace for Productivity, Focus, & Creativity', podcast, 31 January 2022, hubermanlab.com/optimizing-workspace-for-productivity-focus-and-creativity/.

J Meyers-Levy & RJ Zhu, 'The influence of ceiling height: the effect of priming on the type of processing that people use', *Journal of Consumer Research*, vol. 34, no. 2, 2007, pp. 174–186.

G Markowsky, 'Information theory', *Encyclopedia Britannica*, 9 August 2022, britannica.com/science/information-theory/Physiology.

ER Tufte, *Seeing with Fresh Eyes: Meaning, Space, Data, Truth*, Graphics Press LLC, 2020.

M Marsden, interview with author, 2022.

American Academy of Audiology, 'The cocktail party effect', 15 December 2021, audiology.org/the-cocktail-party-effect/.

B Arons, 'A review of the cocktail party effect', *Journal of the American Voice I/O Society*, vol. 12, no. 7, 1992, pp. 35–50.

ML Hawley, RY Litovsky & JF Culling, 'The benefit of binaural hearing in a cocktail party: effect of location and type of interferer', *The Journal of the Acoustical Society of America*, vol. 115, no. 2, 2004, pp. 833–843.

M Toyoda, Y Yokota, M Barnes & M Kaneko, 'Potential of a small indoor plant on the desk for reducing office workers' stress', *HortTechnology*, vol. 30, no. 1, 2019, pp. 1–19.

H Ghanbaran, R Ebrahimpour, P Payedar Ardakani & M Tohidi Moghadam, 'The role of lighting, window views and indoor plants on stress reduction of offices' staffs by psychophysics method', *Iran Occupational Health*, vol. 14, no. 6, 2018, pp. 135–147.

VI Lohr, CH Pearson-Mims & GK Goodwin, 'Interior plants may improve worker productivity and reduce stress in a windowless environment' *Journal of Environmental Horticulture*, vol. 14, no. 2, 1996, pp. 97–100.

KE Lee, KJH Williams, LD Sargent, et al, op. cit.

N Wolny, 'Albert Einstein's messy desk highlights the surprising link between clutter and intelligence', *Entrepreneur*, 15 April 2021, entrepreneur.com/leadership/albert-einsteins-messy-desk-highlights-the-surprising-link/369141.

L Sander, 'The case for finally cleaning your desk', *Harvard Business Review*, 25 March 2019, hbr.org/2019/03/the-case-for-finally-cleaning-your-desk.

CA Roster & JR Ferrari, 'Does work stress lead to office clutter, and how? Mediating influences of emotional exhaustion and indecision' *Environment and Behavior*, vol. 52, no. 9, 2020, pp. 923–944.

TG Horgan, NK Herzog & SM Dyszlewski, 'Does your messy office make your mind look cluttered? Office appearance and perceivers' judgments about the owner's personality' *Personality and Individual Differences*, vol. 138, 2019, pp. 370-379.

S McMains & S Kastner, 'Interactions of top-down and bottom-up mechanisms in human visual cortex', *The Journal of Neuroscience*, vol. 31, no. 2, 2011, pp. 587-597.

BJ Fogg, *Tiny habits: The small changes that change everything*, Eamon Dolan Books, 2019.

How I Work, 'Productivity expert Laura Mae Martin helps you "spring clean" your work habits before returning to the office', podcast, 9 June 2022, amantha.com/podcasts/productivity-expert-laura-mae-martin-helps-you-spring-clean-your-work-habits-before-returning-to-the-office/.

Practice 4: Work in digital dashes

Microsoft, *2022 Work Trend Index: Annual Report*, 16 March 2022, microsoft.com/en-us/worklab/work-trend-index/great-expectations-making-hybrid-work-work.

D Lloyd & EL Rossi (eds), *Ultradian Rhythms in Life Processes: An inquiry into fundamental principles of chronobiology and psychobiology*, Springer-Verlag, 1992.

Med-I-Well, 'Ultradian rhythm & the importance of taking breaks', 21 June 2021, med-i-well.com/inspiration/ultradian-rhythm-the-importance-of-taking-breaks.

G McKeown, *Effortless: Make it easier to do what matters most*, Random House, New York, 2021.

C Newport, *Deep Work: Rules for focused success in a distracted world*, Hachette, London, 2016.

Lizzie Williamson, accessed 21 October 2022, twominutemoves.com.

KE Lee, KJH Williams, LD Sargent, et al, op. cit.

SC Van Hedger, HC Nusbaum, L Clohisy, et al, op. cit.

JP Trougakos, I Hideg, BH Cheng & DJ Beal, 'Lunch breaks unpacked: The role of autonomy as a moderator of recovery during lunch', *Academy of Management Journal*, vol. 57, no. 2, 2014, pp. 405–421.

J Spataro, 'The future of work—the good, the challenging & the unknown', Microsoft blog, 8 July 2020, microsoft.com/en-us/microsoft-365/blog/2020/07/08/future-work-good-challenging-unknown/.

JN Bailenson, op. cit.

C Warhurst, interview with author, 2022.

L Fosslien & MW Duffy, 'How to combat Zoom fatigue', *Harvard Business Review*, 29 April 2020, hbr.org/2020/04/how-to-combat-zoom-fatigue.

H Nesher Shoshan & W Wehrt, op. cit.

G Fauville, M Luo, AC Muller Queiroz, et al, 'Nonverbal mechanisms predict Zoom fatigue and explain why women experience higher levels than men', 2021, papers.ssrn.com/sol3/papers.cfm?abstract_id=3820035.

J Edgar, 'The cosmetic surgery "Zoom boom" is real – but there's more to the story', *Refinery29*, updated 7 October 2021, refinery29.com/en-au/2021/10/10705015/zoom-boom-plastic-cosmetic-surgery-pandemic.

K Johnson, 'It's true. Everyone *is* multitasking in video meetings', *Wired*, 13 May 2021, wired.com/story/stop-looking-your-email-youre-video/.

H Cao, C-J Lee, S Iqbal, et al, 'Large scale analysis of multitasking behavior during remote meetings', *CHI Conference on Human Factors in Computing Systems (CHI '21)*, 8–13 May 2021, Yokohama, Japan, microsoft.com/en-us/research/publication/large-scale-analysis-of-multitasking-behavior-during-remote-meetings/.

K Schoenenberg, A Raake & J Koeppe, 'Why are you so slow? – Misattribution of transmission delay to attributes of the conversation partner at the far-end', *International Journal of Human-Computer Studies*, vol. 72, no. 5, 2014, pp. 477–487.

MW Kraus, 'Voice-only communication enhances empathic accuracy', *American Psychologist*, vol. 72, no. 7, 2017, pp. 644–654.

S Heim & A Keil, op. cit.

Practice 5: Do deep work during peak-performance windows

B Tracy, *Eat That Frog! 21 great ways to stop procrastinating and get more done in less time*, Berrett-Koehler, 2017.

D Pacheco & A Rehman, 'Chronotypes', Sleep Foundation, updated 19 September 2022, sleepfoundation.org/how-sleep-works/chronotypes.

M Breus, *The Power of When: Learn the best time to do everything*, Ebury Digital, 2016.

DH Pink, *When: The scientific secrets of perfect timing*, Riverhead Books, New York, 2018.

A Putilov, N Marcoen, D Neu, et al, 'There is more to chronotypes than evening and morning types: results of a large-scale community survey provide evidence for high prevalence of two further types', *Personality and Individual Differences*, vol. 148, 2019, pp. 77–84.

E Laber-Warren, 'New office hours aim for well rested, more productive workers', *The New York Times*, 24 December 2018, nytimes.com/2018/12/24/well/mind/work-schedule-hours-sleep-productivity-chronotype-night-owls.html.

Future Forum, *Future Forum Pulse Summer Snapshot*, July 2022 futureforum.com/wp-content/uploads/2022/07/Future-Forum-Pulse-Report-Summer-2022.pdf.

F Amini, SM Moosavi, R Rafaiee, et al, 'Chronotype patterns associated with job satisfaction of shift working healthcare providers' *Chronobiology International*, vol. 38, no. 4, 2021, pp. 526–533.

S Cranston & S Keller, 'Increasing the "meaning quotient" at work', McKinsey & Company, 1 January 2013, mckinsey.com/business-functions/people-and-organizational-performance/our-insights/increasing-the-meaning-quotient-of-work.

Dropbox, 'Virtual First Toolkit', accessed 21 October 2022, experience.dropbox.com/virtual-first-toolkit.

C Newport, op. cit.

Eisenhower, 'Introducing the Eisenhower Matrix', accessed 21 october 2022, eisenhower.me/eisenhower-matrix/.

GN Tonietto, SA Malkoc & SM Nowlis, 'When an hour feels shorter: future boundary tasks alter consumption by contracting time', *Journal of Consumer Research*, vol. 45, no. 5, 2019, pp. 1085–1102.

Atlassian, 'My User Manual' accessed 21 October 2022, atlassian.com/team-playbook/plays/my-user-manual.

Practice 6: Mono-task, don't multi-task

V Colliver, 'Prescription for success: Don't bother nurses' *SFGATE*, 28 October 2009, sfgate.com/health/article/Prescription-for-success-Don-t-bother-nurses-3282968.php.

D Gopher, L Armony & T Greenshpan, 'Switching tasks and attention policies', *Journal of Experimental Psychology: General*, vol. 129, no. 3, 2000, pp. 308–339.

U Mayr & R Kliegl, 'Task-set switching and long-term memory retrieval', *Journal of Experimental Psychology: Learning, Memory, and Cognition*, vol. 26, no. 5, 2000, pp. 1124–1140.

University of California - Los Angeles. 'Multi-tasking adversely affects brain's learning, UCLA psychologists report, *ScienceDaily*, 26 July 2006, sciencedaily.com/releases/2006/07/060726083302.htm.

The Economist Intelligence Unit, *In Search of Lost Focus: The engine of distributed work*, 2022, lostfocus.eiu.com.

Dropbox, 'How Dropboxers are taking back the freedom to decline meetings with Core Collaboration Hours', *Medium*, 9 June 2021, medium.com/life-inside-dropbox/how-dropboxers-are-taking-back-the-freedom-to-decline-meetings-with-core-collaboration-hours-3cb9631fb6bf.

J MacKay, 'The state of work life balance in 2019: what we learned from studying 185 million hours of working time', RescueTime blog, 24 January 2019, rescuetime.wpengine.com/work-life-balance-study-2019/.

S Vozza, 'Google's productivity adviser teaches you how to solve your email fatigue', *Fast Company*, 21 May 2021, fastcompany.com/90635338/googles-productivity-advisor-teaches-you-how-to-solve-your-email-fatigue.

A Gupta, R Sharda & RA Greve, 'You've got email! Does it really matter to process emails now or later?' *Information Systems Frontiers*, vol. 13, no. 5, 2011, pp. 637–653.

K Kushlev & EW Dunn, 'Checking email less frequently reduces stress', *Computers in Human Behavior*, vol. 43, 2015, pp. 220–228.

B Hecht, J Teevan & A Sellen, 'The "Leaf Blower Problem" and the importance of common ground', Microsoft, 9 September 2021, microsoft.com/en-us/research/project/the-new-future-of-work/articles/the-leaf-blower-problem-and-the-importance-of-helping-our-users-find-common-ground-in-hybrid-work/.

E(L)J Sander, C Marques, J Birt, et al, 'Open-plan office noise is stressful: multimodal stress detection in a simulated work environment', *Journal of Management & Organization*, vol. 27, no. 6, 2021, pp. 1021–1037.

P Salamé & A Baddeley, 'Effects of background music on phonological short-term memory', *The Quarterly Journal of Experimental Psychology A: Human Experimental Psychology*, vol. 41, no. 1-A, 1989, pp. 107–122.

L Sander, 'Open-plan office noise increases stress and worsens mood: we've measured the effects', *The Conversation*, 5 July 2021, theconversation.com/open-plan-office-noise-increases-stress-and-worsens-mood-weve-measured-the-effects-162843.

id, interview with author, 2022.

H Jahncke, P Björkeholm, JE Marsh, et al, 'Office noise: can headphones and masking sound attenuate distraction by background speech?', *Work: Journal of Prevention, Assessment & Rehabilitation*, vol. 55, no. 3, 2016, pp. 505–513.

JS Jenkins, 'The Mozart effect', *Journal of the Royal Society of Medicine*, vol. 94, no. 4, 2001, pp. 170–172.

Headspace, 'How to Focus While Working From Home | Expert Videos', video, YouTube, 4 November 2020, youtube.com/watch?v=ICtXN_dDyZM.

M Lee, C-B Song, G-H Shin & S-W Lee, 'Possible effect of binaural beat combined with autonomous sensory meridian response for inducing sleep', *Frontiers in Human Neuroscience*, vol. 13, 2019, p. 425.

PILLAR III: DISABLE DIGITAL DISTRACTIONS

The NRMA, *Look up: Keeping pedestrians safe*, June 2019, mynrma.com.au/-/media/documents/advocacy/look-up-keeping-pedestrians-safe.pdf.

R Baron, 'The cockpit, the cabin, and social psychology', accessed 21 October 2022, gofir.com/general/crm/.

BER staff, 'Paying attention: the attention economy', *Berkeley Economic Review*, 31 March 2020, econreview.berkeley.edu/paying-attention-the-attention-economy/.

T Harris, 'It's time to redesign the Attention Economy (Part I)', *Medium*, 10 April 2017, medium.com/thrive-global/its-time-to-redesign-the-attention-economy-f9215a2210be.

HA Simon & A Newell, 'Human problem solving: The state of the theory in 1970 1', in *Structural Learning* (Volume 2), Routledge, 1976.

TED, 'How a handful of tech companies control billions of minds every day | Tristan Harris', video, YouTube, 29 July 2017, youtube.com/watch?v=C74amJRp730.

K Lavinder, 'IQ + EQ = higher performance', ACFE Insights blog, 5 June 2018, acfeinsights.com/acfe-insights/2018/6/5/iq-eq-higher-performance-.

R Holian, 'EQ versus IQ: what's the perfect management mix?', *The Conversation*, 22 July 2015, theconversation.com/eq-versus-iq-whats-the-perfect-management-mix-40001.

The Economist Intelligence Unit, op. cit.

Asurion, op. cit.

Practice 7: Manage your digital load

BrainFacts, 'Hormones: communication between the brain and the body', 1 April 2012, brainfacts.org/brain-anatomy-and-function/cells-and-circuits/2012/hormones-communication-between-the-brain-and-the-body.

R Rubin & D Pfaff (eds), *Hormone/Behavior Relations of Clinical Importance: Endocrine systems interacting with brain and behavior*, Academic Press, 2009.

C Stothart, A Mitchum & C Yehnert, 'The attentional cost of receiving a cell phone notification', *Journal of Experimental Psychology: Human Perception and Performance*, vol. 41, no. 4, 2015, pp. 893–897.

K Neilson, 'How to combat attention residue', *HRM*, 10 November 2020, hrmonline.com.au/section/strategic-hr/how-to-combat-attention-residue/.

S Leroy, 'Why is it so hard to do my work? The challenge of attention residue when switching between work tasks', *Organizational Behavior and Human Decision Processes*, vol. 109, no. 2, 2009, pp. 168–181.

L Corduff, op. cit.

Deloitte, *Media Consumer Survey 2017: Australian media and digital preferences – 6th edition*, 2017, deloitte.com/content/dam/Deloitte/au/Documents/technology-media-telecommunications/deloitte-au-tmt-media-consumer-survey-2017-290818.pdf.

A Haupt, 'Sacrificing sleep to make time for yourself? Tips to stop "revenge bedtime procrastination"', *The Washington Post*, 10 June 2021, washingtonpost.com/lifestyle/wellness/revenge-bedtime-procrastination-meaning-help/2021/06/09/f098af9c-c946-11eb-afd0-9726f7ec0ba6_story.html.

Practice 8: Create more friction

M Baik, H-J Suk, J Lee & K Choi, 'Investigation of eye-catching colors using eye tracking', in *Proceedings Volume 8651, Human Vision and Electronic Imaging XVIII*, 14 March 2013, pp. 192–197.

EJ Masicampo & RF Baumeister, 'Consider it done! Plan making can eliminate the cognitive effects of unfulfilled goals', *Journal of Personality and Social Psychology*, vol. 101, no. 4, 2011, pp. 667–683.

F Gino & B Staats, 'Your desire to get things done can undermine your effectiveness', *Harvard Business Review*, 22 March 2016, hbr.org/2016/03/your-desire-to-get-things-done-can-undermine-your-effectiveness.

AF Ward, K Duke, A Gneezy & MW Bos, 'Brain drain: The mere presence of one's own smartphone reduces available cognitive capacity', *Journal of the Association for Consumer Research*, vol. 2, no. 2, 2017, pp. 140–154.

HH Wilmer, LE Sherman & JM Chein, 'Smartphones and cognition: a review of research exploring the links between mobile technology habits and cognitive functioning', *Frontiers in Psychology*, vol. 8, 2017, p. 605.

LA Manwell, M Tadros, TM Ciccarelli & R Eikelboom, 'Digital dementia in the internet generation: excessive screen time during brain development will increase the risk of Alzheimer's disease and related dementias in adulthood', *Journal of Integrative Neuroscience*, vol. 21, no. 1, 2022, p. 28.

L Dossey, 'FOMO, digital dementia, and our dangerous experiment', *Explore (New York, NY)*, vol. 10, no. 2, 2014, pp. 69–73.

A Sandu & P Nistor, 'Digital dementia', *Eastern-European Journal of Medical Humanities and Bioethics*, vol. 4, no. 1, 2020, pp. 1–6.

J-S Ahn, H-J Jun & T-S Kim, 'Factors affecting smartphone dependency and digital dementia', *Journal of Information Technology Applications and Management*, vol. 22, no. 3, 2015, pp. 35–54.

Practice 9: Minimise your tech temptations

Andrew May, 'Dopamine junkies: constantly seeking… sensation', accessed 21 October 2022, andrewmay.com/dopamine-junkies-constantly-seeking-sensation/ .

A Lembke, *Dopamine Nation: Finding balance in the age of indulgence*, Dutton, 2021.

AM Graybiel & ST Grafton, 'The striatum: where skills and habits meet', *Cold Spring Harbor Perspectives in Biology*, vol. 7, no. 8, 2015, a021691.

LJ Seltzer, TE Ziegler & SD Pollak, 'Social vocalizations can release oxytocin in humans', *Proceedings of the Royal Society B: Biological Sciences*, vol. 277, no. 1694, 2010, pp. 2661–2666.

A Satariano, P Burrows & B Stone, 'Scott Forstall, the sorcerer's apprentice at Apple', *NBC News*, 17 October 2011, nbcnews.com/id/wbna44904886.

N Bowles, 'Is the answer to phone addiction a worse phone?', *The New York Times*, 12 January 2018, nytimes.com/2018/01/12/technology/grayscale-phone.html.

Today, television program, Nine Network Australia, 21 February 2019.

Practice 10: Take peak-performance pit stops

KG Kovvali, *Pit Stops for Peak Performance*, Jaico Publishing House, 2015.

J Guy, 'Employees working from home are putting in longer hours than before the pandemic', *CNN Business*, updated 5 February 2021, edition.cnn.com/2021/02/05/business/working-from-home-hours-pandemic-scli-intl-gbr/index.html.

Qatalog & GitLab, 'Killing Time at Work '22', 2022, language.work/research/killing-time-at-work.

Microsoft, *2022 Work Trend Index: Annual Report*, 16 March 2022, microsoft.com/en-us/worklab/work-trend-index/great-expectations-making-hybrid-work-work.

World Health Organization, 'Long working hours increasing deaths from heart disease and stroke: WHO, ILO', 17 May 2021, who.int/news/item/17-05-2021-long-working-hours-increasing-deaths-from-heart-disease-and-stroke-who-ilo.

F Pega, B Náfrádi, NC Momen, et al, 'Global, regional, and national burdens of ischemic heart disease and stroke attributable to exposure to long working hours for 194 countries, 2000–2016: A systematic analysis from the WHO/ILO Joint Estimates of the Work-related Burden of Disease and Injury', *Environment International*, vol. 154, 106595.

J Korunovska & S Spiekermann-Hoff, *The Effects of Information and Communication Technology Use on Human Energy and Fatigue: A Review*, Working Papers / Institute for IS & Society, 2021.

JN Bailenson, op. cit.

American Psychological Association, 'The American workforce faces compounding pressure: APA's 2021 Work and Well-being Survey results', accessed 21 October 2022, apa.org/pubs/reports/work-well-being/compounding-pressure-2021.

Headspace, 'What Happens to Cause Burnout? Understanding Burnout from Work, Virtual Work From Home and More', video, YouTube, 21 October 2021, youtube.com/watch?v=cFjK5WLpSHE.

Dr Adam Fraser, 'The perfect storm of burnout', 16 November 2021, dradamfraser.com/blog-content/2021/11/16/rechargeable.

id, interview with author, 2022.

P Albulescu, I Macsinga, A Rusu, et al, op. cit.

The E-Lab & Deakin University, op. cit.

D Dorion & S Darveau, 'Do micropauses prevent surgeon's fatigue and loss of accuracy associated with prolonged surgery? An experimental prospective study', *Annals of Surgery*, vol. 257, no. 2, 2013, pp. 256–259.

A Bergouignan, KT Legget, N De Jong, et al, 'Effect of frequent interruptions of prolonged sitting on self-perceived levels of energy, mood, food cravings and cognitive function', *The International Journal of Behavioral Nutrition and Physical Activity*, vol. 13, no. 1, 2016, p. 113.

FS Dhabhar, 'Effects of stress on immune function: the good, the bad, and the beautiful', *Immunologic Research*, vol. 58, no. 2–3, 2014, pp. 193–210.

S Scott, op. cit.

W Hohaia, BW Saurels, A Johnston, et al, 'Occipital alpha-band brain waves when the eyes are closed are shaped by ongoing visual processes', *Scientific Reports*, vol. 12, no. 1, 2022, p. 1194.

W Hof, *The Wim Hof Method: Activate your potential, transcend your limits*, Penguin, 2022.

Tim Ferriss, 'Breathing Techniques to Reduce Stress and Anxiety | Dr. Andrew Huberman on the Physiological Sigh', video, YouTube, 26 October 2021, youtube.com/watch?v=kSZKIupBUuc.

J Fallis, 'The 9 most promising psychobiotics for anxiety', Optimal Living Dynamics blog, 27 April 2022, optimallivingdynamics.com/blog/?author=55832ca0e4b0fe87a727e7ed.

RJ Ellis & JF Thayer, 'Music and autonomic nervous system (dys)function', *Music Perception*, vol. 27, no. 4, pp. 317–326.

Virtusan App, 'Non-Sleep Deep Rest (#NSDR) Protocol - Dr. Andrew Huberman – 10 minute', video, YouTube, 12 September 2022, youtube.com/watch?v=AKGrmY8OSHM.

Tim Ferriss, 'The Practice of Yoga Nidra to Improve Your Sleep and Stress | Dr. Andrew Huberman', video, YouTube, 12 November 2021, youtube.com/watch?v=1rSOn0PurVc.

S Parker, 'Training attention for conscious non-REM sleep: the yogic practice of yoga-nidrā and its implications for neuroscience research', *Progress in Brain Research*, vol. 244, 2019, pp. 255–272.

R Dolgoff-Kaspar, A Baldwin, M Scott Johnson, et al, 'Effect of laughter yoga on mood and heart rate variability in patients awaiting organ transplantation: a pilot study', *Alternative Therapies in Health and Medicine*, vol. 18, no. 5, 2012, pp. 61–66.

L Dexter, K Brook & E Frates, 'The laughter prescription', *American Journal of Lifestyle Medicine*, vol. 10, no. 4, 2016, pp. 262–267.

P Srámek, M Simecková, L Janský, et al, 'Human physiological responses to immersion into water of different temperatures', *European Journal of Applied Physiology*, vol. 81, no. 5, 2000, pp. 436–442.

E Moore, JT Fuller, JD Buckley, et al, 'Impact of cold-water immersion compared with passive recovery following a single bout of strenuous exercise on athletic performance in physically active participants: a systematic review with meta-analysis and meta-regression', *Sports Medicine (Auckland, NZ)*, vol. 52, no. 7, 2022, pp. 1667–1688.

Huberman Lab, 'Dr. Craig Heller: Using Temperature for Performance, Brain & Body Health', podcast, 4 October 2021, hubermanlab.com/dr-craig-heller-using-temperature-for-performance-brain-and-body-health/.

id, 'The science & use of cold exposure for health & performance', 1 May 2022, hubermanlab.com/the-science-and-use-of-cold-exposure-for-health-and-performance/.

S Kang & TR Kurtzberg, 'Reach for your cell phone at your own risk: the cognitive costs of media choice for breaks', *Journal of Behavioral Addictions*, vol. 8, no. 3, 2019, pp. 395–403.

S Sonnentag, 'The recovery paradox: portraying the complex interplay between job stressors, lack of recovery, and poor well-being', *Research in Organizational Behavior*, vol. 38, 2018, pp. 169–185.

LB Steed, BW Swider, S Keem & JT Liu, 'Leaving work at work: a meta-analysis on employee recovery from work', *Journal of Management*, vol. 47, no. 4, pp. 867–897.

LL Ten Brummelhuis & JP Trougakos, 'The recovery potential of intrinsically versus extrinsically motivated off-job activities' *Journal of Occupational and Organizational Psychology*, vol. 87, no. 1, 2014, pp. 177–199.

Roy Morgan, 'It's official: Australians have more annual leave due than ever before', 17 December 2021, roymorgan.com/findings/its-official-australians-have-more-annual-leave-due-than-ever-before.

S Malviya, '6 reasons employees don't use vacation time (and why they should)', Replicon blog, 8 July 2022, replicon.com/blog/6-reasons-employees-dont-use-vacation-time/.

N Beheshti, 'Adam Grant on what the holidays can tell you about burnout' *Forbes*, 22 December 2021, forbes.com/sites/nazbeheshti/2021/12/22/adam-grant-on-what-the-holidays-can-tell-you-about-burnout/?sh=2202705e140f.

Practice 11: Establish power-down rituals

B Van Ark, 'The productivity paradox of the new digital economy', *International Productivity Monitor*, vol. 31, 2016, pp. 3–18.

@lexandra Samuel, 'Meet the dirty digital dozen', *Thrive at Work* email newsletter, us14.forward-to-friend.com/forward/preview?u=75a4fccf122210c2b44821e0f&id=41ec494132.

Cisco, *Employees are ready for hybrid work, are you? Cisco Global Hybrid Work Study 2022*, 2022, cisco.com/c/m/en_us/solutions/global-hybrid-work-study.html.

Headspace, 'How to Focus While Working From Home | Expert Videos', video, YouTube, 4 November 2020, youtube.com/watch?v=ICtXN_dDyZM.

PwC, *Balancing Act: The New Equation in hybrid working*, 2022, pwc.com.au/futureofwork.

L Murphy, *Get Remarkably Organised*. Hachette, 2018.

@glennondoyle, social media post, Instagram, 5 March 2019, instagram.com/p/BumfnYmhEfl/?utm_source=ig_embed&ig_rid=442b4329-c22c-4e62-be3c-a084c7d835fb.

@BreneBrown, social media post, Twitter, 15 June 2018, twitter.com/brenebrown/status/1007412234979545089.

RJ Dwyer, K Kushlev & EW Dunn, 'Smartphone use undermines enjoyment of face-to-face social interactions', *Journal of Experimental Social Psychology*, vol. 78, 2018, pp. 233–239.

J Chu, S Qaisar, Z Shah & A Jalil, 'Attention or distraction? The impact of mobile phone on users' psychological well-being', *Frontiers in Psychology*, vol. 12, 2021, 612127.

S Turkle, *Reclaiming Conversation: The power of talk in a digital age*, Penguin, 2016.

Practice 12: Enjoy mind-wandering mode

MH Immordino-Yang, JA Christodoulou & V Singh, 'Rest is not idleness: implications of the brain's default mode for human development and education', *Perspectives on Psychological Science*, vol. 7, no. 4, pp. 352–364.

C Newport, *Digital Minimalism: Choosing a focused life in a noisy world*, Penguin Random House, 2019.

HG Apostle (ed), *Aristotle's Physics*, Indiana University Press, Bloomington, 1969.

TD Wilson, DA Reinhard, EC Westgate, et al, 'Just think: the challenges of the disengaged mind', *Science*, vol. 345, no. 6192, 2014, pp. 75–77.

C Nederkoorn, L Vancleef, A Wilkenhöner, et al, 'Self-inflicted pain out of boredom', *Psychiatry Research*, vol. 237, 2016, pp. 127–132.

A Hatano, C Ogulmus, H Shigemasu & K Murayama, 'Thinking about thinking: people underestimate how enjoyable and engaging just waiting is', *Journal of Experimental Psychology: General*, 2022, epub ahead of print.

Unlocking Us with Brené Brown, 'Part 5 of 6: Brené with Ashley and Barrett for the Summer Sister Series on The Gifts of Imperfection', podcast, July 2021, open.spotify.com/episode/1FMBgRDdlV2YAP2UkRRhxD.

B Murphy Jr, 'Google says it still uses the "20-percent rule", and you should totally copy it', *Inc.*, 1 November 2020, inc.com/bill-murphy-jr/google-says-it-still-uses-20-percent-rule-you-should-totally-copy-it.html.

D Clark, 'Google's "20% rule" shows exactly how much time you should spend learning new skills—and why it works', *CNBC*, 16 December 2021, cnbc.com/2021/12/16/google-20-percent-rule-shows-exactly-how-much-time-you-should-spend-learning-new-skills.html.

O Burkeman, *Four Thousand Weeks: Time and how to use it*, Jonathan Cape & BH – Trade, 2021.

T Radtke, T Apel, K Schenkel, et al, 'Digital detox: an effective solution in the smartphone era? A systematic literature review', *Mobile Media & Communication*, vol. 10, no. 2, pp. 190–215.

J El-Khoury, R Haidar, RR Kanj, et al, 'Characteristics of social media "detoxification" in university students', *The Libyan Journal of Medicine*, vol. 16, no. 1, 2021, 1846861.

GM Hunt, R Marx, C Lipson & J Young, 'No more FOMO: limiting social media decreases loneliness and depression', *Journal of Social and Clinical Psychology*, vol. 37, no. 10, pp. 751–768.

D Schmuck, 'Does digital detox work? Exploring the role of digital detox applications for problematic smartphone use and well-being of young adults using multigroup analysis', *Cyberpsychology, Behavior and Social Networking*, vol. 23, no. 8, 2020, pp. 526–532.

MMC van Wezel, EL Abrahamse & MMP Vanden Abeele, 'Does a 7-day restriction on the use of social media improve cognitive functioning and emotional well-being? Results from a randomized controlled trial', *Addictive Behaviors Reports*, vol. 14, 2021, 100365.

J Brailovskaia, J Delveaux, J John, et al, 'Finding the "sweet spot" of smartphone use: reduction or abstinence to increase well-being and healthy lifestyle?! An experimental intervention study', *Journal of Experimental Psychology: Applied*, advance online publication.

R Brannigan, CJ Gil-Hernández, O McEvoy, et al, 'Digital engagement and its association with adverse psychiatric symptoms: a longitudinal cohort study utilizing latent class analysis', *Computers in Human Behavior*, vol. 133, 2022, 107290.

A Barasch, K Diehl, J Silverman & G Zauberman, 'Photographic memory: the effects of volitional photo taking on memory for visual and auditory aspects of an experience', *Psychological Science*, vol. 28, no. 8, 2017, pp. 1056–1066.

NM Thomas, SG Choudhari, AM Gaidhane & ZQ Syed, '"Digital wellbeing": the need of the hour in today's digitalized and technology driven world!', *Cureus*, vol. 14, no. 8, 2022, e27743.

S Unrau, social media post, LinkedIn, accessed 21 October 2022, linkedin.com/posts/samantha-unrau-a9793817_probably-the-most-underrated-badass-move-activity-6953754667382161408-aMeZ/.

A Jha, *Peak Mind: Find your focus, own your attention, invest 12 minutes a day*. HarperOne, 2021.

KA Garrison, TA Zeffiro, D Scheinost, et al, 'Meditation leads to reduced default mode network activity beyond an active task', *Cognitive, Affective & Behavioral Neuroscience*, vol. 15, no. 3, 2015, pp. 712–720.

BK Hölzel, J Carmody, M Vangel, et al, 'Mindfulness practice leads to increases in regional brain gray matter density', *Psychiatry Research: Neuroimaging*, vol. 191, no. 1, 2011, pp. 36–43.

JA Brewer, PD Worhunsky, JR Gray, et al, 'Meditation experience is associated with differences in default mode network activity and connectivity', *Proceedings of the National Academy of Sciences*, vol. 108, no. 50, pp. 20254–20259.

JC Basso, A McHale, V Ende, et al, 'Brief, daily meditation enhances attention, memory, mood, and emotional regulation in non-experienced meditators', *Behavioural Brain Research*, vol. 356, 2019, pp. 208–220.

GR Elkins, AF Barabasz, JR Council & D Spiegel, 'Advancing research and practice: the revised APA Division 30 definition of hypnosis', *The International Journal of Clinical and Experimental Hypnosis*, vol. 63, no. 1, 2015, pp. 1–9.

LD Butler, C Koopman, E Neri, et al, 'Effects of supportive-expressive group therapy on pain in women with metastatic breast cancer', *Health Psychology*, vol. 28, no. 5, 2009, pp. 579–587.

J Gruzelier, J Levy, J Williams & D Henderson, 'Self-hypnosis and exam stress: comparing immune and relaxation-related imagery for influences on immunity, health, and mood', *Contemporary Hypnosis*, vol. 18, no. 2, 2001, pp. 73–86.

H Spiegel, 'An eye-roll test for hypnotizability', *American Journal of Clinical Hypnosis*, vol. 53, no. 1, 2010, pp. 15–18.

Conclusion: Your human operating system in action

flight-club, '1 in 60 rule.' video, YouTube, 10 September 2014, youtube.com/watch?v=WiXU2OrDeNo.

B Ware, *The Top Five Regrets of the Dying*, Hay House, 2012.

